解析理查德·J. 艾文斯

《捍卫历史》

AN ANALYSIS OF
RICHARD J. EVANS'S
IN DEFENCE OF HISTORY

Nicolas Piercey　Thomas Stammers ◎ 著

李文中 ◎ 译

上海外语教育出版社
SHANGHAI FOREIGN LANGUAGE EDUCATION PRESS

目 录

引言 1
 理查德·J. 艾文斯其人 2
 《捍卫历史》的主要内容 3
 《捍卫历史》的学术价值 5

第一部分：学术渊源 7
 1. 作者生平与历史背景 8
 2. 学术背景 13
 3. 主导命题 18
 4. 作者贡献 23

第二部分：学术思想 29
 5. 思想主脉 30
 6. 思想支脉 36
 7. 历史成就 41
 8. 著作地位 45

第三部分：学术影响 51
 9. 最初反响 52
 10. 后续争议 57
 11. 当代印迹 62
 12. 未来展望 67

术语表 71
人名表 75

CONTENTS

WAYS IN TO THE TEXT	83
Who Is Richard J. Evans?	84
What Does *In Defence of History* Say?	86
Why Does *In Defence of History* Matter?	88
SECTION 1: INFLUENCES	91
Module 1: The Author and the Historical Context	92
Module 2: Academic Context	98
Module 3: The Problem	104
Module 4: The Author's Contribution	110
SECTION 2: IDEAS	115
Module 5: Main Ideas	116
Module 6: Secondary Ideas	123
Module 7: Achievement	129
Module 8: Place in the Author's Work	134
SECTION 3: IMPACT	141
Module 9: The First Responses	142
Module 10: The Evolving Debate	147
Module 11: Impact and Influence Today	153
Module 12: Where Next?	158
Glossary of Terms	163
People Mentioned in the Text	167
Works Cited	172

引 言

要 点

- 理查德·J. 艾文斯是英国历史学家,出生于1947年,其学术声誉主要来自于他对德意志帝国和纳粹德国*的研究,还有在历史学方法(历史学领域的研究和分析方法)方面的各种论著。

- 《捍卫历史》(1997)成书的背景是"客观*真理"以及西方传统历史学方法受到质疑,而这种质疑是后现代主义*的典型理念。该书为历史学研究、写作以及学习过程中追求准确性和中立性提供了有力的辩护。

- 在这部研究历史编纂学*方法和目标的著作中,艾文斯将历史学的发展描绘为一种学术实践,他以自己研究的实例来证明,历史学在社会科学中仍占有一席之地。

理查德·J. 艾文斯其人

《捍卫历史》(1997)的作者理查德·J. 艾文斯,是当今英国最重要的德国史专家之一。他1947年出生于伦敦东北部郊区的伍德福德,在牛津大学学习历史期间,师从多位当代最伟大的历史学家,并对历史方法论产生了浓厚的兴趣。历史学家 E. H. 卡尔*的重要学术专著《历史是什么?》深深吸引着他,在艾文斯的著作中该书的影响清晰可见。艾文斯受围绕弗里茨·菲舍尔*的争论的启发,决定专注于德国社会史*研究。弗里茨·菲舍尔是一位历史学家,他坚持认为德国导致了第一次世界大战*的爆发。艾文斯在斯特林大学、东英吉利大学和伯贝克学院(伦敦大学)均担任讲师职位,其发表的有关德国女权主义*、刑事司法和公共卫生的研究专著都备受好评。

在伯贝克教学期间，艾文斯决定出版《捍卫历史》，对史学领域中后现代主义分析方法的发展和影响提出警告。后现代主义是一种与当代艺术和文化分析相关的运动，通常表现为质疑客观性，认为所有解读同等有效。作为一个专注研究现代德国的历史学家，艾文斯意识到这种理论框架存在潜在危险。尽管他之前曾专门写过批判第三帝国*（1933年由阿道夫·希特勒和纳粹党创立的政权，一直持续到1945年第二次世界大战*结束）的德国历史学家，但是在《捍卫历史》中艾文斯是第一次探讨有关史学方法的更宽泛的问题。

艾文斯在纳粹主义研究方面具备专业知识，因而被指定为"欧文—利普施塔特"诽谤案的证人。在该案中，英国学者大卫·欧文*起诉美国历史学家黛博拉·利普施塔特*诽谤并败诉。艾文斯的证词对于揭露欧文是"大屠杀*否定者"（大屠杀为第二次世界大战期间，纳粹德国对数百万欧洲犹太人的工业化灭绝）至关重要。

2008年，艾文斯被聘为剑桥大学历史学钦定讲座教授，并在他的就职演讲中，颂扬英国前辈历史学家致力于欧洲大陆研究的学术传统（演讲内容在2005年出版为《大都会岛民》一书）。作为第三帝国崛起和消亡的最新三部曲的作者，艾文斯获得了诸多荣誉，被任命为剑桥大学沃尔夫森学院院长，2012年被英国女王授予爵士头衔。

《捍卫历史》的主要内容

在《捍卫历史》中，艾文斯试图对抗后现代主义理论对历史学实践所构成的威胁。

历史学是否可以成为具有清晰规则并能预测未来结果的学科？它是否具有客观性（摆脱个人偏见，辨别"真实"现象的可能性）？这些辩论并不新鲜。事实上，艾文斯对英国历史学家 G. R. 埃尔顿*和 E. H. 卡尔在 20 世纪 60 年代有关这些问题的辩论深感兴趣。但是，由于受新兴语言观的影响，目前对历史学研究方法的质疑已被置于一个新的立足点。这种语言观有时被称为批评理论的"语言学转向"*，最初是由文学评论家和哲学家提出来的，如法国思想家罗兰·巴特*和雅克·德里达*。

这些理论家认为，词语的意义并不是固定在其所指的对象或概念上，而是通过与词语和其他能指符号的差异及关系发生作用，如通过声音和意象指向各种意义。因此，不能将历史事件视为仅具有唯一的、固定的意义或单一的解读。基于这些见解，思想家和学者如历史学家和文化评论家海登·怀特*认为，历史写作与文学创作并没有根本不同，因为不同的历史学家可以研究相同的历史事件，并得出不同的结论和解读。英国后现代历史学家基思·詹金斯*进一步指出，文献记录不可能面面俱到，也不可能绝对公正，因此历史学家不可能通过这些文献而得知有关过去的"真相"。

这种观点直击历史学作为独立学科的立身之本，质疑其方法、目的以及呈现真相的意图。

艾文斯接受挑战，多方面驳斥后现代主义的观点。首先，他通过对历史学科发展的重新描述，表明围绕客观性、原始材料选择及表述的政治性这些问题的争论并不新鲜；历史学作为一门学科，一直以来比后现代主义者认为的更多样化，更具自我批判精神，也更激进。其次，他坚持认为后现代主义者对文本和语言的主张在概念层面上缺乏内在的一致性，可能导致他们自己的研究实践无效（那些后现代主义假设本身并不可靠，并可能导致历史学家无法进行正确分析）。第三，艾文斯强调，后现代主义对客观可能性的怀疑论调，导致了无法预料的社会和政治后果。他认为，如果没有判断真相或准确性的标准，各种扭曲或反动思想就会大行其道，包括否认大屠杀的言论。

值得注意的是，他批判的主要目标不是后现代主义哲学家，而是那些试图引用这些观点来颠覆历史书写方法的历史学家。

艾文斯对后现代主义者关于真理、因果和客观性的立场进行反驳，他的基本策略是以实例为论据，而不是基于各种抽象的语言学理论。后现代主义有可能会彻底破坏历史学学科内部通用的研究方法和证据规范，众多历史学家对此忧心忡忡，此时艾文斯对追求客观性的辩护广受欢迎。尽管传统的评论家和后现代主义评论家都批评《捍卫历史》，但该书在商业上大获成功，迄今已再版 11 次，并被译成多种欧洲和亚洲语言。该书所受到的关注，深刻揭示了历史研究方法和动因的持续发展的过程。

《捍卫历史》仍是一本介绍方法论争议的好书（"方法论争议"即关于历史研究和分析方法的争论，在 20 世纪末一度盛行于历史学领域）。

《捍卫历史》的学术价值

《捍卫历史》在思想上并不具有革命性，该书之所以能够卓然而立，在于它能激发我们去思考应该如何研究历史，在于它以一种独特的方式向读者介绍了众多不同的思想家和历史学家，从传统的经验主义*学者（他们相信知识的权威性建立在可以通过观察验证的证据基础上）到后现代主义学者。该书描绘了自 20 世纪 60 年代以来历史学科的演变，涵盖了多种社会史（专注于社会各个方面的历史研究）。艾文斯还利用他个人对现代德国历史的研究来说明他特有的研究方法。他能够以一种简单和引人入胜的方式讨论复杂和宽泛的问题，这使他的表达方式几乎与其著作中包含的思想一样重要；他以一种立论有据、平易近人的修辞方式来反驳晦涩难懂的后现代主义理论。尽管他强调客观性，但这并不妨碍他对同行进行非常主观和批判性的说明。《捍卫历史》还展示了一场活力四射，甚至极具说服力的辩论秀。

此外，艾文斯的公众形象，以及他多次作为历史记忆和纳粹主义遗留问题专家公开露面，表明了他的研究方法的影响远远超出了学术界。艾文斯在"欧文—利普施塔特"诽谤案的庭审中出庭作证，强调了对过去的事件进行准确和可验证的呈现是多么重要。在随后的著作中，他进一步反思了历史学家的公共职能和公民职能，展示了如何通过学术研究帮助大众了解过去。

尽管艾文斯对历史学中的客观性、主观性（解读受个人感受或预设的影响）以及因果关系的认知方式依然存在不少问题，但正如该书书评所言，《捍卫历史》激发并扩大了争论。该书从2000年版开始，增加了内容翔实、观点激进的后记，这表明艾文斯在该书中提出了诸多关于研究方法和道德方面的重要问题。其根本问题在于，客观的历史真相是不是人们想要的，乃至人们能够想象的？艾文斯在书中成功并令人信服地论证道，虽然主观性肯定会影响历史学家的解读，但历史的客观性仍值得追求。

第一部分：学术渊源

1 作者生平与历史背景

要点

- 《捍卫历史》仍然是前代学者对史学方法的研究中最有影响力和最清晰的论著之一。
- 艾文斯早已成为一位受人尊敬的社会历史学家,这使他能够对最近的历史趋势作权威性的评论。
- 艾文斯的写作背景是经典马克思主义*解读——基于政治理论家和经济学家卡尔·马克思的分析方法而创立的解读——的衰落以及高等教育机构面临的新压力。

为何要读这部著作?

基于一系列讲座,理查德·J.艾文斯在1997年9月出版了《捍卫历史》。该标题反映了20世纪80年代末和90年代初期在学术界形成的一种合理焦虑。特别是它试图捍卫历史研究实践,以抗击艾文斯所认为的极端后现代主义(一种艺术和文化分析运动,质疑在文学和社会科学诸领域中各种根深蒂固的假设)的威胁和后现代主义思想对学术的客观性、事实的中立性以及历史学的科学属性等概念所提出的挑战。

在该书中,艾文斯试图展示历史学作为了解过去的一种手段所具有的活力,同时捍卫严谨的史学方法的重要性。艾文斯指出,在20世纪90年代中期,历史学经历了来自后现代思想家的严峻挑战,包括历史学家基思·詹金斯、海登·怀特和历史哲学家弗兰克·安克斯米特*。

对于历史研究方法如何演变,艾文斯提供了一个简要而有影响力的说明。他认为历史学家确实能够找到过去所发生事件的"真相",即使这种真相总是局部的和暂时的。艾文斯激起了很多争论,以至于该书促使人们开始反思,历史学家到底能从后现代主义学到些什么。

> "在这个意义上,历史学家如何获得关于过去的知识,以及他们是否能够完全实现自己的志业,就成了一个更大问题的引子,即对于我们时代的重大议题,整个社会在多大程度上能够确实地掌握它们的客观情况,从而使我们敢于在面对21世纪的人类未来时,作出性命攸关的抉择。"
>
> ——理查德·J. 艾文斯:《捍卫历史》

作者生平

理查德·J. 艾文斯是一位职业历史学家。他于1947年出生在伦敦郊区的伍德福德,其父亲是附近一所学校的教师。[1] 他的父母在20世纪初经济衰退(俗称"大萧条"*)期间从威尔士的一个小村庄搬迁到伦敦。[2] 艾文斯于1966年前往牛津耶稣学院学习现代史。在牛津大学学习期间,艾文斯开始接触英国马克思主义历史学家(遵循政治理论家及经济学家卡尔·马克思分析理论的历史学家)的思想,同时也接触了年鉴学派*(一个极具影响力的历史学派,致力于研究社会各个方面,而不是仅仅关注精英人士)以及主办《历史工场*期刊》的激进团体(一个历史学家团体,在目标和方法上赞同马克思主义学者和年鉴学派的主张)。[3] 他参加过著名历史学家克里斯托弗·希尔*、基思·托马斯*和休·特雷弗-罗珀*的讲座。1969年,艾文斯毕业并获得优等荣誉学位,随后前往牛津大学圣安东尼学院攻读博士学位，致力于研究20世纪初的德国女权主义运动。

在完成学业后，艾文斯在斯特林大学和东英吉利大学担任讲师。1989年至1998年间，艾文斯担任伦敦大学伯贝克学院历史系教授，他在那里撰写了《捍卫历史》并于1997年出版；2008年至2014年担任剑桥大学近代历史学钦定讲座教授。

在政治上，艾文斯基本上算是中间偏左派，他在大学期间曾受到马克思主义和左翼思想的影响。

艾文斯最著名的学术贡献是他对纳粹德国和大屠杀的研究，包括他的《第三帝国三部曲》[4]和他的《希特勒的阴影》[5]对战后德国史学的研究。2000年，艾文斯作为法律辩护的专家证人参加了英国作家大卫·欧文诉美国历史学家黛博拉·利普施塔特诽谤案的庭审，后者曾经把欧文称作"大屠杀否认者"。[6]这一事例表明，艾文斯在历史分析中坚持真理和客观性的立场具有重要的现实意义，这一立场认为并非所有解读都同样有效（正如否认大屠杀案所清晰表明的），而且历史证据可以用来确定某一事件的事实。

创作背景

20世纪后期，学者们围绕历史学在当代学术界中的作用展开了激烈的争论，一些学者甚至提出整体解散历史学科。20世纪80年代至90年代，一大批后现代主义者批评了关于知识权威的传统观念，特别是批评了西方视角的主流地位，甚至提倡相对主义*的立场，认为任何历史学家都无法对过去建立一种单一的、客观的"真相"。

尽管这些观点在执业历史学家中并不常见，但激进的怀疑论在历史学和历史编纂学理论家群体中仍然蓬勃发展。在一批法国思想家（如文学理论家罗兰·巴特、社会理论家米歇尔·福柯*和哲学家雅克·德里达等）的推动下，人文学科中的批评理论在20世纪80年代和90年代得到了显著的发展，与之相伴的是冷战*结束后政治和意识形态的转向（冷战指美国及其盟国与苏联*及其盟国之间的长期紧张局势，始于第二次世界大战之后，并于20世纪的最后十年结束）。

与此同时，许多后现代主义者开始质疑关于世界普遍真理的宏大叙事，一些后现代主义核心观念逐渐取代了马克思主义的首要地位，而马克思主义分析方法和政治立场曾为许多社会历史学家提供了指导框架。

这种知识界的转变与高等教育的广泛调整也密切相关。20世纪60年代和70年代，历史系和执业历史学家的总数迅速扩增；但到了20世纪80年代，这种趋势被逆转，这是由于当时英国和美国的右翼政府上台并削减了大学的经费。这一挫折直接导致了历史学家们的薪酬、独立性和地位的下降，而根据艾文斯的说法，历史研究这一专业有分裂为多个互不相干领域的危险。[7]在拒绝客观真理的同时，后现代主义者声称历史学家倾向于传播那些更能迎合当权者需要并反映其价值观的历史版本，从而忽视那些被边缘化者的观点。尽管艾文斯强烈反对后现代主义者对历史学科更为极端、更总体性的观点，但他的确承认，关于应该如何研究、书写和教授历史的辩论对于20世纪90年代的英国具有独特的意义和价值。[8]

1. 了解理查德·J.艾文斯的个人信息，可浏览他的网站：http://www.richardjevans.com。
2. 丹尼尔·斯诺曼："丹尼尔·斯诺曼见证的德国历史学家——欧文案中的专家证人和历史的捍卫者"，《今日历史》，2004年第54期，第45页。
3. 理查德·J.艾文斯："评论：年鉴学派：安德雷·伯格尔的思想史"，《伦敦书评》第31卷，2009年第23期，第12—14页。
4. 理查德·J.艾文斯：《第三帝国的到来》，伦敦：艾伦·莱恩出版社，2003年；《当权的第三帝国（1933—1939）》，伦敦：艾伦·莱恩出版社，2005年；《战争中的第三帝国（1939—1945）》，伦敦：艾伦·莱恩出版社，2008年。
5. 理查德·J.艾文斯：《希特勒的阴影：西德历史学家和逃离纳粹历史的尝试》，纽约：万神殿出版社，1989年。
6. 黛博拉·利普施塔特：《审判中的历史：我与大卫·欧文在法庭上的一天》，纽约：哈珀永久出版社，2006年。
7. 理查德·J.艾文斯：《捍卫历史》（第2版），伦敦：格兰塔出版社，2001年，第171—173页。
8. 艾文斯：《捍卫历史》，第179页，第205页。

2 学术背景

要点 🔑

- 历史学理论和历史编纂学（对历史学家的目标和方法的研究）都考虑了历史学科的演变。

- 保守的"实证主义"学者倾向于认为历史学家可以通过研究历史文献来准确地重构过去；与此相反，那些受到后现代主义思潮影响的学者则否认重构过去客观知识的可能性，因为所有历史学家都通过他们自己的文化成见、预设及偏见来解读他们手头的文献。

- 理查德·J.艾文斯试图在二者之间找到平衡点，他认为尽管历史学家某种程度的主观性（不可能不偏不倚地进行分析）是不可避免的，但文献证据可以提供可验证的事实，以约束对过去事件的解读。

著作语境

理查德·J.艾文斯的《捍卫历史》主要针对那些后现代主义思想家，他们对能否对过去事件进行权威性解读以及客观性概念本身提出根本性挑战，从而对历史的独立学科地位产生质疑。在19世纪初期，在德国历史学家利奥波德·冯·兰克*的倡导下，历史学被置于一种更严谨、更科学的地位。兰克坚持认为，通过严格调查和对比档案材料，历史学家将能够看到过去"真实的情况"。兰克和他的支持者普遍坚持政治史和外交史的首要地位，并致力于研究和理解政治家们的行为和决策。[1] 然而，19世纪和20世纪的许多学者认为，历史学家应该同样关注统治精英阶层之外的各个社会群体、各种经济模式以及更广泛的文化生活。

后现代主义思想运动所提出的一些问题，如历史学家对过去事件的扭曲、叙事的不可靠性等，可能看起来很新颖，但实际上这种质疑已有数百年历史。艾文斯说："两千五百年前，希腊历史学家修昔底德*在他的《伯罗奔尼撒战争史》的序言中抱怨诗人们和其他人正在对所发生的事情进行虚假和虚构的描述，并表明自己的意图就是要正本清源。"[2] 然而，这与20世纪80年代的后现代主义挑战是截然不同的，因为后者攻击历史的客观性，攻击在历史分析中得出"真理"的可能性，而这些攻击与新的语言学理论有关。许多后现代主义思想家坚持认为，词语（或"能指"）的意义不是通过它们与世界上的对象和概念的固定关系获得意义，而是通过它们与其他词的关系和差异获得意义。受法国思想家如罗兰·巴特和米歇尔·福柯的影响，后现代主义者进一步认为意义是由读者产生的；据此，读者在文本中发现的东西远比作者的意图更重要。

他们认为，真理永远不会是绝对的或普遍的，真理总是局部的或偶然的（依赖于某些预设或视角），而历史文献就像任何其他文本一样，都是开放性的，可以被无限地解读。艾文斯写作《捍卫历史》，就是为了表明这种观点对历史学家的危险性。

> "历史理论太重要了，怎能完全交给理论家呢。上天可能没有赐予从事实际研究的历史学家以机敏的辩才，但是，他们与其他人一样，完全具有思考和写作的权利，而且他们所具备的实际研究经验，理应使他们能够作出自己特有的贡献。"
>
> ——理查德·J.艾文斯：《捍卫历史》

学科概览

艾文斯在《捍卫历史》的开头不走寻常路，他不是先讨论最近的后现代思想家，而是从更早一代的辩论开始。德裔英国历史学家 G. R. 埃尔顿和英国马克思主义历史学家 E. H. 卡尔在 20 世纪 60 年代对历史研究方法有着截然不同的观点，埃尔顿支持历史文献的绝对权威，而卡尔拒绝经验主义——主张任何论点都应建立在通过观察证明的证据之上，而不是基于某种历史理论——并赞同档案证据与现实关注具有相互作用。尽管二者观点相左，但艾文斯显然对他们都很钦佩。与抽象地研究历史方法的后现代历史学家基思·詹金斯不同，卡尔和埃尔顿都在研究档案和文献而积累的经验中磨炼了自己的哲学见解。

我们可以将研究历史方法问题的学者大致划分为三种不同的类型。第一类是传统的、但人数不断减少的经验主义者，如埃尔顿。他们相信，埋头于历史文献，从而获得关于过去的客观知识是可能的。第二类包括了绝大多数的历史学家，诸如卡尔和艾文斯，他们在不同程度上相信通过历史研究了解过去是可能的，但这种了解总是零散的、不完整的，并且受到历史学家对于现实关注的影响。第三类为新潮的理论家或后现代主义者，其中包括荷兰历史学家弗兰克·安克斯米特和詹金斯，他们普遍认为，历史学无法对过去事实提供客观公正的描述。对于后现代主义者而言，历史写作是当下占统治地位的群体的一种建构。

学术渊源

《捍卫历史》直接模仿了 E. H. 卡尔 1961 年的经典作品《历史

是什么?》。艾文斯借用了卡尔的许多章节标题,该书的最后一段更是"对卡尔末段的模仿"。[3] 卡尔对艾文斯史学思想的主要影响是他断言历史是过去和现在之间的对话。历史不是完全由文献证据构建的,也不是完全来自历史学家个人的主观认知,而是来自两者之间的相互作用。卡尔还想扩大历史研究的范围,使之超越精英阶层和世界领袖。但艾文斯还对卡尔著作中的虚伪选择提出了批评,指出卡尔"绝对清楚那些(在他看来)对激发历史变革贡献很少或无所贡献的人,如女性,或处于原始状态、缺乏政治组织的群众,并不值得历史学家关注。"[4]

此外,艾文斯关注卡尔思想中的目的论*假设(假设历史可以被认为是出于特定目的的一系列事件)。卡尔认为,唯一值得书写的历史发展,是那些成功扰乱现在或改变未来的发展。艾文斯认识到这种思想具有"极其令人不安"的含义,因为它可能导致历史学家不再讲述失败的事迹,或忽略被边缘化的群体。[5]

同样,艾文斯不完全赞成卡尔对因果关系的决定论*观点(如他认为在某种条件下,某些事件是不可避免的),不赞同他支持借自社会科学的模型,也不认同他对历史学家预测能力的信念。[6] 作为卡尔的崇拜者,艾文斯也努力展示了他与前人的不同之处。

---

1. 理查德·J. 艾文斯:《捍卫历史》(第2版),伦敦:格兰塔出版社,2001年,第16—19页。
2. 艾文斯:《捍卫历史》,第260页。

3. 艾文斯:《捍卫历史》,第 269 页。
4. 艾文斯:《捍卫历史》,第 212 页。
5. 艾文斯:《捍卫历史》,第 269—270 页。
6. 艾文斯:《捍卫历史》,第 138 页,第 73 页。

3 主导命题

要点

- 在20世纪后期,执业历史学家和批评理论家——基本上是指在哲学、文学和社会科学方面进行跨领域研究的思想家——质疑历史能在多大程度上客观真实地描述过去,甚至试图否定历史的客观性。
- 后现代文学评论家相信文本只能指涉其他文本;后现代主义思想家,如历史学家海登·怀特和基思·詹金斯,将这一原则用于历史学,声称历史写作只涉及历史学家和现在。
- 艾文斯利用他自己的历史研究实例来重述该学科的历史,以期为史学的存在价值和历史写作中的客观性追求提供理据。

核心问题

理查德·J.艾文斯的《捍卫历史》涉及到主体性的基本问题,即历史分析不可能不受历史学家的社会背景和个人偏见的影响。历史在多大程度上可被视为客观和真实的?历史写作实践与其研究对象——也就是过去——具有多大的关联?本质上,这些问题探讨了历史学家是否能够捕捉和表现实际发生过的事情,或者他们是否仅仅是参与了一项实践,该实践不是揭示过去事件,而更多地是展现他们自己的现实想象力和文化背景。这个问题对于历史学的有效性至关重要,无论其作为一个研究领域,还是一门研究学科。如果像一些后现代主义者所说的那样,过去是无法再现的,那么作为研究过去的历史学在概念上就站不住脚,其当前形式的学科就已经完结。客观性、真实性和准确性对历史学家而言是基本概念,《捍卫历史》的宏旨就是坚持这样一种主张，即历史学家能够并且应该寻求过去的真相，即使这种真相是不完善的。

尽管这些辩论代表了20世纪后期后现代主义思想兴起的一个显著方面，但这些问题并不新鲜。正如艾文斯所言，历史学的科学性或客观性对于该学科在19世纪的形成至关重要。在20世纪60年代，经验主义历史学家埃尔顿和相对激进的马克思主义历史学家卡尔就"历史学家如何开展研究"以及"历史学家能够知道什么"这些问题因观点不同而展开论争。到了20世纪80年代，当后现代主义理论新的形式出现，并在历史学和历史编纂学的各种新兴研究哲学中成为潮流时，卡尔和埃尔顿给出的答案就难以为继了。

哲学和批评理论中的"语言学转向"强调语言在所有形式的文化分析中的作用，基于该观点，后现代主义者挑战"历史文献是透明的，并指向客观的外在现象"这一基本前提；相反，他们认为历史学在本质上是主观的，是在历史学家的思想中构建的，反映了历史学家的文化背景。后现代主义思想确实鼓励采用更广泛和更具包容性的方法来呈现历史证据并与之互动，艾文斯也承认了这一点。[1]但他觉得有必要撰写《捍卫历史》，以警示他所认为的一些后现代哲学可能带来的更危险的影响，如忽视严谨性、作者公然的党派之争以及道德相对主义（认为道德判断实际上是不可能的，因为我们不能真正把握道德层面上的任何事情）。

> "我们可以通过感官系统去感受和体验当下的真实；但过去已经不复存在，它不像此刻环绕在我们周围的这个世界那样的'真实'。过去已成为文本。"
> ——理查德·J. 艾文斯：《捍卫历史》

参与者

后现代主义对历史学提出挑战的思想渊源可以追溯至20世纪60年代后期出现的文学批评。在法国，罗兰·巴特和雅克·德里达等语言理论家颠覆了关于语言和意义的传统观念。在巴特的论文《作者之死》（1977）中，他驳斥了这样一种观点，即读者可以完全破译或还原作者的初始意图。对于巴特而言，意义是通过阅读和解读获得的，而不是由作者意图最终确定的。[2] 巴特还指出，传统历史学家认为过去有待发现，而他自己则把历史叙事看成由各种文学和学术策略创造的"结果"。[3]

同样，被称为"解构主义"*的思想运动强调了这样一种理论，即我们对世界的认识完全是由语言调节的。正如德里达和其他解构主义者所断言的那样，意义来自语言符号之间的相互作用；因此，很难想象有什么东西存在于"文本之外"。读者的解读，而不是作者的意图，才是最终产生意义的所在。[4]

历史学家海登·怀特、弗兰克·安克斯米特和基思·詹金斯把这些观点扩展并应用到了历史学中。海登·怀特指出，历史和所有文学一样，都是一种建构，并且同样依赖于叙事。对于怀特来说，在历史方法的范围内，有多种同样可行的方式来表述过去。[5] 詹金斯认为，历史学是一种栖身于特定意识形态中的话语，即构成"文本"的一套陈述和预设系统；詹金斯辩称，历史学家与其研究过去，还不如研究其他历史学家都说了些什么。[6] 像怀特一样，安克斯米特提出历史是一种建构，历史著作之间的差异不在研究实践，而只是写作风格不同。[7] 与研究过去相比，历史学应该关注过去在当下是如何被表述的。

这些后现代主义思想从根本上质疑历史学的目的和有效性。《捍卫历史》试图回归到这样一种观念，即历史文本与现实具有根本的关联性，严谨性、公正性和客观性原则仍然应该是执业历史学家的追求。

当时的论战

后现代主义思想家（特别是那些在自己的著作中很少使用严谨的历史方法的后现代主义思想家）对历史学家不屑一顾，艾文斯对此十分不满。为了反驳他们的指责，艾文斯广泛地吸收了前人的思想，包括埃尔顿和卡尔在20世纪60年代的学术辩论；艾文斯甚至追溯到英国历史学家G. M. 特里维廉*，他是19世纪末和20世纪初社会史的先驱实践者。

《捍卫历史》充分地阐述了历史学在19和20世纪的发展历程，并据此反驳所谓"历史学在本质上已经不复存在"这种后现代主义观点。他展示了历史学家所涉及的一系列主题和使用的方法，很有说服力地回击了后现代主义者的嘲讽——后现代主义者讽刺历史学家只是一个关注精英的单一群体。艾文斯有力的论证中不乏机智，他通过引用19世纪历史学家关于技巧的辩论，揭穿了后现代主义多个观点的虚假新颖性，如要求历史学家更多地关注受压迫群体："当后现代历史学家在20世纪90年代中期推崇'重新发现历史的失败者'时，人们不禁怀疑，他过去30年来到底一直生活在哪个星球上。"[8] 在讨论像"客观性"这种复杂的哲学概念时，艾文斯借鉴了当代美国历史学家彼得·诺维克*和托马斯·哈斯克尔*就客观性与中立性之间微妙差异的辩论。[9]

艾文斯为探讨客观性这一重要概念，提供了大量历史理论的例子，并着重强调学者之间的著名争论，如20世纪50年代英国历史学家劳伦斯·斯通*和休·特雷弗-罗珀之间关于斯通对17世纪英国贵族地位的文献证据的解释的争论，以及20世纪80年代美国历史学家大卫·亚伯拉罕*关于大企业和希特勒崛起之间众说纷纭的联系的争论。

---

1. 理查德·J.艾文斯：《捍卫历史》（第2版），伦敦：格兰塔出版社，2001年，第248页。
2. 罗兰·巴特："作者之死"，载《图像、音乐、文本》，伦敦：丰塔纳出版社，1977年，第142—148页。
3. 艾文斯：《捍卫历史》，第94页。
4. 雅克·德里达：《语法学》，加亚特里·C.斯皮瓦克译，马里兰州巴的摩和伦敦：约翰·霍普金斯大学出版社，1997年；艾文斯：《捍卫历史》，第94—95页。
5. 海登·怀特：《元史学：19世纪欧洲的历史想象》，马里兰州巴尔的摩和伦敦：约翰·霍普金斯大学出版社，1975年；艾文斯：《捍卫历史》，第100—101页。
6. 基思·詹金斯："历史是什么？"，《从卡尔和埃尔顿到罗蒂和怀特》，伦敦：路特雷奇出版社，1995年；艾文斯：《捍卫历史》，第97页。
7. F. R. 安克斯米特：《历史表现》，加利福尼亚州斯坦福：斯坦福大学出版社，2002年。
8. 艾文斯：《捍卫历史》，第213页。
9. 艾文斯：《捍卫历史》，第116—123页。

4 作者贡献

要点

- 后现代主义思想提出了"历史研究中不可能存在客观性"的挑战，而艾文斯极具创造性地应对了这一挑战。他通过历史实践表明，某种形式的客观性是必要的和可能的。
- 艾文斯利用他自己以前研究大屠杀的理论成果，抨击了后现代主义的政治虚伪性。
- 他对历史学进行了全面的概述，同时表明了后现代主义的益处和危害。

作者目标

理查德·J. 艾文斯的《捍卫历史》直接应对来自后现代主义思想的批评。虽然一些执业历史学家认为这些论点无足轻重，但艾文斯认为这是一种自满的态度，尤其是考虑到这些论点在本科课程中所产生的巨大影响。艾文斯毫不含糊地指出："历史学理论太重要了，怎能完全交给理论家呢"，[1]并试图说服读者"要捍卫历史研究这项学术事业，我们应该坦率地直面极端怀疑论者，与之辩论，而不是简单地视而不见，或一骂了之。"[2]

在反对极端后现代主义观点的论辩中，艾文斯既要展示后现代主义概念中的内在矛盾，还要表明坚持极端相对主义立场的危险性，极端相对主义认为任何一种关于过去的认知版本都是有效的。

期望详细拆解后现代主义哲学的读者也可能会误解这本书的目标。虽然艾文斯反对极端的后现代主义理论，但这种对抗仅限于历史研究实践，而不是试图做出更大的哲学干预。《捍卫历史》的目的之一就是叙述历史学发展的各个阶段，从最初强调政治史的首要地位，到20世纪60年代和70年代向经济史、社会史和文化史的扩展。艾文斯表明，历史学家对自己的方法比那些批评者所说的更具自我意识。为了说明这一点，他引用了自己的研究实例。例如，为了回应后现代主义历史学家海登·怀特的观点，即历史学本质上是一种文学形式，艾文斯讲述了他自己的主要著作《汉堡之死》是如何出于"美学"上的考虑构建了"十二个平行叙事"，以便既要以一种"最令人兴奋和最有趣的方式"呈现材料，又要基于对历史事实的严谨研究。[3] 对于艾文斯来说，认为"历史学家是天真的"或者"历史学家不愿意反思他们在构建历史事实中的积极作用"的说法是完全不真实的。

> "然而，对历史学家而言，收起通往自己学科堡垒的吊桥并不是明智之举……历史学家应该更加有区别地对待汹汹入侵的符号学家、后结构主义者、新历史主义者、福柯论者、拉康主义者等。他们有些乍看是敌人，其实何妨当作良师益友呢。"
>
> ——理查德·J. 艾文斯：《捍卫历史》

研究方法

艾文斯把"对于历史学家来说是否可能有客观性"这一哲学问题与特定的社会和政治背景联系起来。他驳斥了英国后现代主义历史学家基思·詹金斯提出的论断，即历史学家只是通过各种机构——特别是大学——参与到主流价值观的重建中。他通过展示历史学家——特别是社会历史学家——的许多研究实例来反驳詹金斯，社会历史学家们力图揭示过去的不公正现象并记录被压迫群体的困境，如工人阶级、妇女和性少数群体。[4]

他通过引用马克思主义和女权主义（倡导两性平等的行动和理论）指出，对历史变迁的元叙事*——以非常广阔的视角说明历史潮流，揭示历史发展方向——绝非天生反动（反对社会进步）。此外，他还质疑后现代主义是否真正像它假装出来的那样进步和激进。最后，艾文斯质问道：如后现代主义所断言，如果在判断历史的不同版本时根本无客观性可依，无法超越道德或审美偏好，那么后现代主义是否在"为任何想要压制、歪曲或掩盖过去的人提供借口"？[5]

艾文斯从他研究德国史深厚的功底中汲取批判的力量。20世纪80年代，在一场名为"史家之辩"*的激烈论战中，历史学家通过与其他独裁政权的大屠杀政策对比，就大屠杀的特异性以及重构或从道德上理解纳粹罪行的困难性等问题争论不休。艾文斯密切地观察了这场争论，他在《现代史学期刊》的一篇文章中阐述了自己的观点，即社会史有助于人们从道德层面理解大屠杀这一时期。[6]这场辩论向艾文斯清楚地证明了讨论客观性的利害关系，同时也表明了一些后现代主义者所暗示的"历史的各种版本并无分别"这一观点有极大危害性。

时代贡献

《捍卫历史》就像卡尔的《历史是什么?》，来自作者所作的一系列讲座。[7]艾文斯确认，他于20世纪90年代在英国伯贝克学院学习期间形成了对历史知识、客观性和真理性的思想。他的观点属于历史主流，并且在许多方面接近其他20世纪90年代重要的历史实证研究学者，如英国历史学家约翰·托什*和鲁德米拉·乔丹诺娃*。艾文斯审慎地强调，他的著作不是在为任何一个学派辩护，而是提倡多元的历史研究路径。与埃尔顿或美国历史学家格特鲁德·希梅尔法布*这样的传统主义者——他们捍卫客观性是为了回归精英主义政治历史——不同，艾文斯极为赞同自20世纪60年代和70年代以来历史学家对所关注话题的拓宽。艾文斯主张各种实证方法，同时呼吁对许多不同类型的历史研究多"一点思想上的宽容"。[8]

与埃尔顿这样对社会史怀有敌意的传统主义者不同，艾文斯在当代发展中看到了许多积极因素。新的贸易和交流机会正在创造一个"国际化的思想市场"以及对世界历史勃然而兴的兴趣。[9]艾文斯对后现代主义的观点绝不是完全否定的。例如，后现代主义强调叙事和风格的重要性，这有助于"重新认可优美文笔其实是合理的历史实践"，如罗伯特·达恩顿*和娜塔莉·泽蒙-戴维斯*等文化历史学家富有想象力的著作呈现的那样，后者是20世纪80年代畅销书《马丁·盖尔归来》的作者。[10]艾文斯欢迎后现代思想的一些元素，而这些元素要么已经与历史学长期以来的自我审视相媲美，要么可以有益地融入历史研究实践中。《捍卫历史》旨在消除后现代主义那些更具破坏性的因素，因为这些因素有可能会颠覆历史学中有关真实性的概念。

---

1. 理查德·J.艾文斯：《捍卫历史》（第2版），伦敦：格兰塔出版社，2001年，第14页。
2. 艾文斯：《捍卫历史》，第255页。

3. 艾文斯:《捍卫历史》,第 146 页。
4. 艾文斯:《捍卫历史》,第 20—68 页。
5. 艾文斯:《捍卫历史》,第 232—233 页。
6. 理查德·J. 艾文斯:"新民族主义和旧历史:对西德史家之辩的看法",《现代历史期刊》第 59 卷,1987 年第 4 期,第 761—797 页。
7. 丹尼尔·斯诺曼:"丹尼尔·斯诺曼见证的德国历史学家——欧文案中的专家证人和历史的捍卫者",《今日历史》,2004 年第 54 期,第 47 页。
8. 艾文斯:《捍卫历史》,第 182 页。
9. 艾文斯:《捍卫历史》,第 177 页。
10. 艾文斯:《捍卫历史》,第 244 页。

第二部分：学术思想

5 思想主脉

要点 🗝

- 艾文斯的主要目的是捍卫历史研究实践中的弱客观性概念,将历史视为"弱"科学而非"硬"科学。
- 历史学方法是确定过去真实情况的重要手段;虽然历史学家无法绝对确定过去的真相,但他们可以通过以严谨的学术态度研究历史文献来逼近真相。
- 艾文斯刻意以一种清晰而令人愉悦的方式写作,以便与他的后现代主义论敌使用的术语形成鲜明对比,并能让普通读者更好接受。

核心主题

在《捍卫历史》的绪论中,理查德·J.艾文斯概述了有关历史学科现状的各种争辩,并提到一些极端后现代主义者的观点,他们质疑历史学及其未来作为研究领域的有效性。艾文斯表明,这本书的核心目的是捍卫历史学免受这些批评的攻击,并以此拯救这个学科。他通过回顾历史学科在近代的演变来达成这一目标。

艾文斯首先确认,19世纪历史学家利奥波德·冯·兰克较早倡导材料分析,这具有重要意义,接着艾文斯描绘了随着历史学家开始关注来源更加丰富多样的原材料,如外交公文、政府会议纪要和统计记录等,客观性观念逐步形成。[1]在20世纪60年代,历史研究视野进一步拓宽,历史学吸纳了那些被忽视和被排斥群体的文献资料,并将兰克的价值观与进步政治学和全球历史观点结合起来,深具社会历史学背景的艾文斯对此持欢迎态度。[2]《捍卫历史》的基础在于，艾文斯致力于从历史的视角去思考历史学实践本身。他声称，后现代主义史学家的弱点之一，是他们不愿意对自己强施于人的立场进行"自我反思"，这表明后现代主义在历史学批判中的一个关键缺陷，就是它所信奉的相对主义很容易被用来破坏自己的立场。[3]

艾文斯回应了这样一种说法，即历史学固有的主观性使它无法成为一门科学。他断言历史学是一门"弱"科学，不像物理学、化学和生物学那样的硬科学，这些领域由精确的定律所支配，以确保在实验环境中具有高度预测力。艾文斯进一步阐述自己的观点："如果历史学家试图预测未来，这种做法肯定是错误的。生活不像科学，总是充满了太多的意外。"[4] 尽管历史学不是基于某种定律，足以使历史学家可靠地预测未来，但它有一套标准、方法和知识体系，以使其研究实践变得科学。它还可以得出有关过去的可验证的通则。艾文斯总结说，历史是科学、艺术和技艺的混合体。[5] 他表明优秀的历史学家不是简单地再现社会主流思想，而是通过对严谨性和准确性的追求，"揭露流行的历史神话中之陈词滥调。"[6] 在进行公正而彻底的研究时，历史学使我们接近过去事件的真相，即使这种真相总是近似的——"获得一些站得住脚的结论，即便这些结论仍有探讨空间。"[7]

> "历史文献的语言从来不是透明的，历史学家早就意识到，不可能仅靠语言，就洞察其背后的历史真实。历史学家们知道，而且一直都知道，我们只能来'透过一层深色玻璃'察看过去，这无需后现代主义现身指出来。后现代主义所做的，不过是将关于历史文本及材料的透明性或模糊性之类我们熟知的见解，置于一种二元对立、非此即彼的极端局面之下。"
>
> ——理查德·J. 艾文斯：《捍卫历史》

思想探究

艾文斯相信，某种形式的客观性是可能的，因为历史文本与过去的现实相联系，通过比较和检验，历史学家可以破译哪些来源是可靠和有启发性的。基于文献的历史研究实践约束了历史学家对过去事件的描述，由此艾文斯指出，后现代主义理论家的暗示是错误的，他们认为历史学家可以自由地杜撰或构建过去发生的事件。然而，他也承认，历史学家会将自己的想法带入他们的研究中，并且不能完全独立于他们自己的文化背景。艾文斯认同马克思主义历史学家卡尔，提出历史学家"不仅仅是听取证据，而且与之对话，积极地对其质询，并用其检验在当今提出的理论和思想。"[8] 依此核心概念，艾文斯坚持认为历史学是一门具有持久相关性的真正学科。[9]

在阐述观点时，艾文斯尽可能利用历史研究实践中所产生的问题，基于这些具体的实例作出论断，而不是诉诸抽象的理论演绎。在回顾 G. R. 埃尔顿和 E. H. 卡尔关于研究和分析方法的争论时，艾文斯将他们的哲学观及历史研究联系起来。埃尔顿提出了一个经验主义论断，即历史文献及其所包含的事实本身就能说明问题。艾文斯揭露了埃尔顿历史实践中的一个盲点，表明由于埃尔顿不愿意考虑现实背景的作用，所以自己的一些偏见得不到正视。一个典型的例子就是英国历史上都铎时代（1485—1603）对强势政府的偏好，艾文斯认为这实际反映了埃尔顿的当代关注。[10] 与此相反，卡尔认为历史学家的工作就是从当前的视角回顾过去，以确定哪些因素和事件对人类进步的贡献最大；他对马克思主义的信仰使他将"客观性"与为捍卫苏联的进步事业而写作等同起来。

虽说学者直接承认自己的政治立场不无益处，但危险的是，这可能左右历史学家对其主题的处理，也就是说，它可能产生巨大的影响。在艾文斯看来，卡尔的左翼政治倾向使他的历史著作在任何反对 1917 年俄国革命的团体眼里都变得不可容忍，在这场革命中，俄国的统治者沙皇被推翻，共产党政府成立。[11] 这些实例展示了艾文斯如何力图超越陈旧的、有缺陷的客观性概念，同时表明从历史实践中可以吸取哪些教训，以回应后现代主义的挑战。

对于艾文斯而言，支持客观性的历史学家既富有想象力，又受现有证据局限的约束，同时还要抵制其个人的政治或道德立场的侵扰。虽然过去的历史总是暂时的、不完整的，并且受当前外部理论的指导，但当历史学家在选择和分析历史材料时，客观性就悬停于他们自己的道德或政治议程中。[12]

语言表述

艾文斯的著作广征博引，并晓畅易懂。由于该书形成于他在伦敦伯贝克学院讲授的课程，所以它旨在以清晰和易懂的方式介绍历史学科中的重大问题，如历史事实、因果关系和客观性。[13] 除了使该书尽可能地顺达和通透，艾文斯的写作风格还体现了一种策略，即突显他自己与那些后现代主义者的不同之处。在他看来，后现代主义者"发展出一套深奥的专业语言和术语，它们主要借自文学理论，这使他们的文章除了其他后现代主义者之外，任何人都无法读懂。"艾文斯抓住了后现代主义者的晦涩难懂的写作弊病，来证明他们的"自恋"和"精英主义"。[14]

艾文斯虽然赞成后现代主义者对措辞的讲究，但提倡历史学家应"坚持一种朴素的风格，除非他们完全清楚自己在做什么"，因为他们每说一个论点，都应该是为了"澄清而不是混淆"。[15] 艾文斯很乐意指出那些由于历史学家误用语言而导致的粗陋或混乱。事实上，艾文斯文章的趣味之一，就是他攻击批评对象时所展示出来的不留情面的幽默。他在书中往往对史学领域往日的大名人殊无敬意，包括休·特雷弗-罗珀（艾文斯引用了他关于"非洲野蛮部落毫无历史价值的轮转更替"的无礼评论）和20世纪早期的历史学家G. M.特里维廉（艾文斯注意到他"对历史上社会地位低下的人表现出家长式和居高临下的姿态"）。[16] 艾文斯尤其不能原谅后现代主义批评家的马虎大意。例如，在回应美国历史学家乔伊斯·阿普尔比*的批评时，他指出："她甚至故意错误地引用了书名，说明她的学术标准存在问题。"[17] 这种坦率而刺耳的旁白使这本书读起来令人欲罢不能。

---

1. 理查德·J.艾文斯：《捍卫历史》（第2版），伦敦：格兰塔出版社，2001年，第110—111页。
2. 艾文斯：《捍卫历史》，第196—198页。
3. 艾文斯：《捍卫历史》，第115页。
4. 艾文斯：《捍卫历史》，第62页。
5. 艾文斯：《捍卫历史》，第66页。
6. 艾文斯：《捍卫历史》，第207页。
7. 艾文斯：《捍卫历史》，第253页。
8. 艾文斯：《捍卫历史》，第230页。
9. 艾文斯：《捍卫历史》，第73页。
10. 艾文斯：《捍卫历史》，第230—231页。
11. 艾文斯：《捍卫历史》，第226—228页。

12. 艾文斯:《捍卫历史》,第 239 页。
13. 艾文斯:《捍卫历史》,第 257 页。
14. 艾文斯:《捍卫历史》,第 200 页。
15. 艾文斯:《捍卫历史》,第 69 页。
16. 艾文斯:《捍卫历史》,第 163 页,第 178 页。
17. 艾文斯:《捍卫历史》,第 256 页。

6 思想支脉

要点

- 艾文斯声称,后现代主义思想运动的确能为历史书写带来一些好处,但他同时指出夸大个人和个人主体性(如个人信仰和历史背景带来的偏见)作用的危险性。
- 历史研究的不断扩展和多样化有可能破坏历史学的单一学科性,但艾文斯对共同标准的长远意义持乐观态度。
- 对于艾文斯来说,后现代主义思想适用于某些时期和问题而不是全部领域。

其他思想

理查德·J.艾文斯的《捍卫历史》特别关注后现代主义对社会历史的影响。"语言学转向"的影响——在文化分析的多个领域,人们越来越重视语言对于理解"真相"的重要性——使得主流历史书写愈来愈突出和关注边缘群体。艾文斯作为一名社会历史学家,其早期研究兴趣集中在19世纪德国女性和罪犯的经历,这使得他对后现代主义在历史研究实践方面的影响持欢迎态度。[1] 与后现代主义者一样,他对上一代历史学者的褊狭和欧洲中心*式的傲慢(指一些学者心胸狭隘,固守历史研究建立在欧洲视角之上的观念)甚为不满。[2] 他还认识到,后现代主义有助于强调普通人在历史中的重要性。他引用了影响力很大的19世纪政治理论家卡尔·马克思的格言:"人民创造了自己的历史,但他们并不是在他们自己选定的条件下创造的。"[3]

虽然后现代主义肯定有助于社会史的发展，但艾文斯还是指出它有可能会受到不当使用。它的理念可能会被"推得太远"，导致"我们只能获得另外一种思想上的简化论，代替社会经济上的简化论。"[4] 换言之，他认为后现代主义的危险是要使个人解读的作用无可非议，而忽视更广阔的社会背景和共同的文化真理的作用。

对个人身份过分重视还会带来另外一个危险。后现代历史学家过于喜欢说"我"，在描述过去时公开地诉诸自己的经验和观念，并且强调同理心的核心作用。[5] "其最终含义就是，每个人只了解他自己的个体身份，除此之外一无所知。经验是真理的唯一仲裁者。"[6] 对于艾文斯而言，这种观点是危险的，因为它表明只有女性才能写出女权主义者的历史，或者只有法国历史学家才能写法国的历史。这一立场令人担忧，因为它剥夺了被压迫者去讲述压迫者故事的机会，并掩盖了这一事实：优秀的历史书写意味着在很大程度上需要那些"明显的他者"和那些"看似熟悉的"共同参与。[7]

> "历史追寻真正'科学'如同追逐海市蜃楼。在催生新方法和新技术这点上，这种追求还是非常有益的……历史学不仅仅是一种严格来说较弱的科学，它还是（或者可以是）一门艺术，也就是说，在某些高手手中，它能够以文学形式和语言呈现，不逊色于其他任何文学作品，且能备受欢迎。"
>
> ——理查德·J. 艾文斯：《捍卫历史》

思想探究

为了证明他的"后现代主义者嘲讽了历史学家"这一观点，艾文斯阐述了该学科的现状。他表明，自20世纪60年代，由于多所大学新成立了历史系，该专业大规模扩张。与扩张相伴的，是社会史研究成为热潮,并导致人们越来越关注以前被主流历史学家所忽视的群体和个人。[8]对于老一代历史学家所奉行的社会史模式而言,这是一个显著的进步。例如,尽管卡尔一直研究俄国革命,但是他坚持认为,群众只有在政治上组织起来并推动进步的事业时,才值得在历史书写中受到重视。[9]

这种狭隘的态度现在已被颠覆。妇女历史、黑人历史、同性恋历史、微观历史和文化历史都在蓬勃发展。艾文斯赞同这种历史思想中的民主化。"如今几乎所有对当代人类有意义或重要性的事物都有了书面历史,当然,这指的是对所有各色人等都重要,而不仅仅是对一小部分有教养、有权力的精英。"[10]

尽管如此,这种扩张并非没有危险。随着一系列子领域和子专业的发展,人们最初期待社会史可以提供一种"整体史"的统括形式,如今这种希望破灭了。如果每个子领域都有自己的研究问题和优先关注点,那么"单一的历史学科还能存在"的观点就越来越难以令人信服。彼得·诺维克是一位以历史理论著称的学者,他认为历史已经过于碎片化,以至于那个拥有自己规范和目标的单一学者社群已不复存在。[11]相比而言,艾文斯更乐观一些。电子通信和频繁的国际旅行使世界各地的学者更容易分享思想。此外,尽管历史学家所使用的理论有所分歧,但变得越来越重要的事情是,他们必须共同遵守一种通用的征引和呈现证据的方式。与后现代主义者的怀疑相反,艾文斯坚持认为,"解读的确是可以通过证据来检验并证实的……证明孰对孰错也是完全可能的。"[12]

被忽视之处

艾文斯通过运用他在德国史方面的专业知识表明,将所有历史解读视为同等有效会带来何种严重后果。艾文斯讨论了后现代主义观念如何被用来为否认大屠杀找借口，他得出的结论是，像其他新的历史学方法一样，后现代主义理论可能只在某些历史学领域更适用。[13] 艾文斯认为，忽视真相的理论用之于大屠杀这种事件，就会使纳粹主义及其受害者变得无足轻重。他引用专门研究德国纳粹历史的学者简·卡普兰*的观点，后者声称对于涉及到近来人们生老病死的历史问题，不能如此傲慢地应用后现代主义理论。[14] 尽管艾文斯认为在大屠杀问题上使用后现代主义理论是不恰当的，但他没有提出更广泛的问题：某些理论或历史学方法是否更适合特定的历史时期或历史事件？

这是一个具有重要意义的问题。如果后现代主义理论不适合讨论大屠杀，那么还有哪些时期或主题也不能应用后现代主义思想？如果真是这样的话，我们该使用什么标准来确定这一点，那么这种标准还能适用于哪些理论或历史时期？这是否只与研究者可获得的资源有关，或与相关事件的道德性有关？

然而，这些微妙的概念点被那些评论家错失了，他们因为自己对史学理论的评论被人与否认大屠杀相关联而恼羞成怒。20世纪80年代，围绕重新发现的比利时文学评论家保罗·德曼*的战时反犹太主义*言论引发了争论，这一争论暴露了他的解构主义理论中"开脱罪责的潜台词"（也就是说，这暴露了他的反犹主义情绪可能已经影响了他的理论观点，因为他的理论可以用来质疑那些记载在案的、可怕的历史事件的"真相"）；考虑到这一背景，我们应能理解艾文斯是完全会引用"否认大屠杀"来佐证其研究的。[15]

1. 理查德·J.艾文斯:《德国女权运动（1894—1933）》,伦敦：圣哲出版社,1976年；《惩罚的仪式：德国死刑史（1600—1987）》,牛津：牛津大学出版社,1996年。
2. 理查德·J.艾文斯:《捍卫历史》(第2版),伦敦：格兰塔出版社,2001年,第178页。
3. 艾文斯:《捍卫历史》,第189页。
4. 艾文斯:《捍卫历史》,第186页。
5. 艾文斯:《捍卫历史》,第200页。
6. 艾文斯:《捍卫历史》,第211页。
7. 艾文斯:《捍卫历史》,第214页。
8. 艾文斯:《捍卫历史》,第162页,第171页。
9. 艾文斯:《捍卫历史》,第164页。
10. 艾文斯:《捍卫历史》,第165页。
11. 艾文斯:《捍卫历史》,第176页。
12. 艾文斯:《捍卫历史》,第128页。
13. 艾文斯:《捍卫历史》,第243页。
14. 艾文斯:《捍卫历史》,第242—243页。
15. 艾文斯:《捍卫历史》,第234页。

7 历史成就

要点

- 艾文斯成功引起人们关注历史学的重要性以及对客观性的追求；《捍卫历史》吸引了大量读者，并在许多国家取得了商业上的成功。
- 这本书也受到了后现代主义追随者的激烈批评。
- 艾文斯的写作风格清晰而富有吸引力，并深植于史学实践中的实例。

观点评价

理查德·J. 艾文斯的《捍卫历史》在很大程度上实现了自己的目标。尽管该书的内容受到了传统和后现代主义思想家的批评，但艾文斯成功地阐释了"为什么历史是一个有效的学术领域"和"为什么要捍卫历史"的个人观点；这本书已成为许多大学本科学生的标准史学教材，特别是在美国和英国。该书于1997年、1998年分别以精装本和平装本发行，很快被翻译成意大利语、德语、瑞典语、土耳其语、日语和韩语。评论家普遍认为，该书内容全面，论点说服力强，同时极富趣味性，尤其喜欢把他的对手像烤串儿一样串起来批驳。正如《柯库斯评论》所指出的那样，艾文斯"将他的同行——无论其是活着的还是过世的，左翼还是右翼，北方的还是南方的——都一一带到摔跤台上，并欢快地将许多人撂倒在地。"[1]

在2000年版中，艾文斯声称"本书的主要目标之一就是激发辩论"，在这一点上，他当然也是成功的。[2] 艾文斯回忆说，这本书所获得的报道数量非同寻常，引起了"远超我预期的评论"。[3] 不同领域、不同意识形态立场的人对艾文斯的方法和结论纷纷提出质疑和挑战，以至于他花费数年时间通过历史研究所的在线论坛分别予以回复，之后才在 2000 年版的《后记》中正式回应各种批评。

> "后现代主义理论家和批评家完全有理由要求历史学家重新思考他们的工作所要处理的分类和预设，并证明他们在实践其学科时采取的方法是行之有效的。后现代主义本身就是众多理论中的一组，并且与其他理论一样，都是可以争论的。就我个人而言，我仍然乐观地认为客观的历史知识既可期待，又可实现。"
>
> ——理查德·J. 艾文斯：《捍卫历史》

当时的成就

在 20 世纪后期，英国大学的知识氛围直接成就了《捍卫历史》。它成书于艾文斯所说的学术界左派陷于混乱和"无能"之际，而这种混乱和无能又因随之而来的"学术界危机而突显，这场危机肇始于 20 世纪 70 年代，并在 20 世纪 80 年代达到了顶峰"。[4] 艾文斯能够表明，后现代主义就是这段过渡时期的产物，他向同行们保证，后现代主义将很快蜕变为历史学的子领域或子专业，"而不是对历史学的理论和实践带来整体上的革命性变化。"[5] 该书尽管总是与具体的时间和地点联系在一起，但涉猎广博，其核心论题又是关于历史学有效性的普遍问题，因此对学生、教师和广大公众都非常有用。

艾文斯立场的基石是他断言，如何处理历史材料具有超越学术的重要意义。引人注目的是，艾文斯在 2000 年历史学家黛博拉·利普施塔特被控诽谤案中作为专家证人出庭作证，对大屠杀否认者大卫·欧文进行了抗辩。《捍卫历史》认为利普施塔特是研究否认大屠杀的"主要权威",艾文斯认同她的担忧,即阴谋论和"修正主义"(挑战历史正统观念)在20世纪90年代的美国大行其道,而当时"诘责西方理性主义传统的做法蔚然成风"。[6] 在庭审中,他被要求评论欧文的研究在历史上是否准确。艾文斯谴责欧文,表明欧文对大屠杀的描述经受不住学术诚信的考验,并认为利普施塔特的指控是合法的。对于艾文斯来说,试图援引后现代主义理论作为否认大屠杀的借口是徒劳的。艾文斯坚持认为,"奥斯威辛不是话语。""如果将大规模谋杀视为一种文本,那无异于对大屠杀视而不见。"[7]

局限性

尽管《捍卫历史》本来也可适用于其他被后现代主义挑战其思想和惯例的领域,如文学研究、艺术、经济学、语言学、建筑学和哲学,但艾文斯并没有就此全面探讨后现代主义思想家的哲学思想。对许多人来说,其著作的主要弱点就在于未能全面分析对手的观点。英国文学评论家斯特凡·科里尼*在《卫报》上写道,该书的分析失于肤浅,其特点是"对庸俗思想的庸俗反驳"[8]。然而,艾文斯将这种批评视作恭维:"如果他说的庸俗意思是'通俗'的话,那我将欣然接受批评。"[9] 他的书不是写给那些理论领域的专家读的,而是写给那些把理论概念延伸应用于自己的研究实践上的人,也是写给那些圈外的读者,他们看不懂后现代主义思想家使用的专业而又晦涩难懂的语言。艾文斯对后现代主义行话的厌恶,促使他将这些复杂的论辩转化为更容易理解的语言,并以更透明的方式挑战它们。但科里尼认为,艾文斯希望受欢迎的愿望是以牺牲对后现代主义哲学的严肃探讨为代价的,这种观点也不无道理。

不出所料,一些学科的学者们——这些学科(如文学研究)与解构主义(认为意义取决于语言的文化分析方法)以及后现代主义比较相容——抱怨说艾文斯没有充分讨论他们所批评的理论家。凯瑟琳·贝尔西*是一位受人尊敬的当代哲学诠释者,她指责艾文斯一边在宣扬仔细阅读的优点,一边却在实践中误解并误用了一些作家的深刻思想,如哲学家雅克·德里达和文学理论家罗兰·巴特。对于贝尔西来说,艾文斯抛弃了对这些思想家真正的理解,他宁愿把他的对手呈现为一系列"妖怪"或"知识怪物,以吓唬那些耳根软的人"。[10]

---

1. "理查德·艾文斯——《捍卫历史》",《科克斯书评》,1998年11月1日,登录日期2015年7月23日,https://www.kirkusreviews.com/book-reviews/richard-j-evans/in-defence-of-history/.
2. 理查德·J.艾文斯:《捍卫历史》(第2版),伦敦:格兰塔出版社,2001年,第316页。
3. 艾文斯:《捍卫历史》,第254页。
4. 艾文斯:《捍卫历史》,第198页。
5. 艾文斯:《捍卫历史》,第203页。
6. 艾文斯:《捍卫历史》,第241页。
7. 艾文斯:《捍卫历史》,第124页。
8. 斯特凡·科里尼:"真相破坏者",《卫报》,1997年12月18日,第15页。
9. 艾文斯:《捍卫历史》,第256页。
10. 凯瑟琳·贝尔西:"捍卫历史",《欧洲英语研究期刊》第3卷,1999年第1期,第108页。

8 著作地位

要点 🗝

- 艾文斯的历史研究主要涉及德国近代史，但他在讨论历史研究方法时使用了更广阔的视野。
- 《捍卫历史》在很大程度上得益于他早先对德国社会史的研究，同时这一研究背景也对他之后成为公共历史学家产生了影响。
- 最近，艾文斯在《大都会岛民》（2005）中扩展了他反对民族主义的立场，该书研究了20世纪英国欧洲历史实践的传统。

定位

《捍卫历史》于1997年9月出版，当时理查德·J. 艾文斯50岁，已经出版了许多历史著作，主要关注德国近代史。他在牛津大学读书时，就特别关注有关弗里茨·菲舍尔著作的争论，菲舍尔是一位历史学家，认为德国人应对第一次世界大战的爆发负责。[1] 艾文斯对社会史产生了浓厚的兴趣，他的第一本书《德国的女权主义运动（1894—1933）》（1976）对这一领域研究作出了重大贡献。[2] 他的主要著作《汉堡之死》（1987）论述了1830年至1910年间该市霍乱病疫爆发对社会和政治造成的影响，[3] 而《惩罚的仪式》（1997）则讨论了1600年至1987年间的德国的死刑制度。[4]

德国社会史的研究背景是《捍卫历史》的写作基础，这使得艾文斯可以有力地驳斥后现代主义对大屠杀研究所产生的影响。同样地，后现代主义者认为，传统历史总是"赢家的故事"，经常忽略被边缘化群体的叙述。艾文斯认为这种概括是不切实际的，并指出"正是穷人和那些名不见经传者、失败者,甚至是女性,吸引了最多的历史学家,并且成为绝大多数书籍的主题。"⁵ 自 1997 年出版《捍卫历史》以来,艾文斯越来越远离对 19 世纪后期德国的研究,并出版了关于纳粹德国的三部曲巨著。⁶ 但他继续关注并研讨历史编纂学问题,这些问题不仅影响到其他德国史学家,也影响到该学科关涉的所有成员。艾文斯被任命为剑桥大学历史学钦定讲座教授,作为其中的一个必要环节,他于 2009 年以"英国历史学家的欧洲大陆研究"为主题——他自身对这一研究传统作出了显著贡献——发表了就职演讲。⁷

> "彻底的相对主义不能提供一种客观标准来证明法西斯主义和种族主义的历史观是错误的……自 20 世纪 70 年代中期以来,大屠杀否认者活动的广度和强度都在增加,这反映了后现代主义思想气候的猖獗,尤其是在美国,在这种氛围中学者们越来越否认文本具有任何固定的意义,甚至认为其意义都是由读者赋予的,诘责西方理性主义传统的做法风行一时。"
>
> ——理查德·J. 艾文斯:《捍卫历史》

整合

在 20 世纪 70 年代,艾文斯与其他多位年轻的英国社会历史学家一道,对关于威廉二世德国*(1871—1918)的既定观点提出了挑战。⁸ 艾文斯等英国社会历史学家使德国史研究的焦点从高层政治、国家和普鲁士对其他日尔曼邦国的统治,转向更复杂的社会关系。⁹ 该群体受到"新左派"*的影响,新左派是一场知识分子运动,主张"自下而上看历史"¹⁰(对之前被视为无关紧要的个人和团体进行研究）。艾文斯的历史方法中有一部分是强调"政治基层组织和普通人的日常生活及经验的重要性"。[11] 为驳斥"后现代主义为被压迫者提供了新的干预"的观点,艾文斯在《捍卫历史》中明确表示,社会史已经在实践中承担起了揭露"社会不平等基本结构"的使命。[12]

德国的历史也为艾文斯提供了这样一种例证,表明为什么公平地研究历史是一个公民责任问题。他参加过"史家之辩"("史家之辩"由保守派历史学家挑起,他们想挑战多数德国人的"内疚感"),并由此观察到,那些与客观性和同情心相关的学术问题具有怎样的政治敏感性。在《希特勒的阴影》(1989)中,艾文斯谈到了多位德国历史学家在阐述纳粹政权的遗产时所感到的尴尬,再次强调了他们作为学者影响公众观点的潜力。[13] 这一观点在《捍卫历史》中有所体现,因为艾文斯担心后现代主义可能会破坏历史学家寻求和表达真相的社会义务,在 2000 年否认大屠杀的作家大卫·欧文败诉的诽谤案审判中,艾文斯以专家证人的身份出席庭审时就表述了这一观点。次年,他反思了这一案件,并为此写作了《为希特勒说谎》,希望将这一认识扩及公共领域中的历史学家。[14]

意义

《捍卫历史》仍可见于许多大学的阅读书目中,这说明了该书的持久影响力。该书迄今已印刷 12 次了,还被翻译成 12 种语言,这清楚地证明了它的意义不仅仅局限于英国。尽管在传统历史学派和后现代主义历史学家那里受到了大量的批评,但艾文斯几乎没有改变他的立场。事实上,他在这本书 2000 年版附加的一篇措辞严厉的《后记》中直接回应了他的批评者们。与《汉堡之死》等他早期的社会史研究著作相比,《捍卫历史》并不那么受学者们的尊重,但毫无疑问它是艾文斯所有作品中读者群最为广泛、争议最为激烈的一本书。他在2001年为卡尔《历史是什么?》四十周年纪念版所写的导言,就是对自己著作持久影响力的庆贺。[15]

后现代主义挑战在20世纪90年代似乎极具威胁性,却在随后的十年中基本消失了。但艾文斯在《捍卫历史》中反对的一些立场又重新出现了。艾文斯尖锐地批评了知识分子的民族主义,抨击了G. R. 埃尔顿的假设,即历史学家应该专注于撰写本民族或国家的历史。艾文斯感叹道,在研究其他文化时,德国和法国的历史学家依旧表现得"顽固且封闭",也就是说,在研究其他文化时他们不知放眼世界。与此相比,艾文斯赞扬了英美学者的贡献,他们撰写了研究其他国家的重要历史著作。[16]

这一主题在他2009年的著作《大都会岛民》中得到了再次体现。在此,艾文斯赞扬那些将深度研究与可读性及写作技巧结合起来的英语学者所取得的成功,并警告说,由于学校外语教学的衰落,可能会产生一种新的知识孤立主义。[17]

---

1. 丹尼尔·斯诺曼:"丹尼尔·斯诺曼见证的德国历史学家——欧文案中的专家证人和历史的捍卫者",《今日历史》,2004年第54期,第45页。
2. 理查德·J. 艾文斯:《德国女权主义运动(1894—1933)》,伦敦:圣哲出版社,1976年。
3. 理查德·J. 艾文斯:《汉堡之死:霍乱时期的社会和政治(1830—1910)》,牛津:克拉伦登出版社,1987年。

4. 理查德·J. 艾文斯：《惩罚的仪式：德国死刑史（1600—1987）》，牛津：牛津大学出版社，1996 年。
5. 理查德·J. 艾文斯：《捍卫历史》（第 2 版），伦敦：格兰塔出版社，2001 年，第 212 页。
6. 理查德·J. 艾文斯：《第三帝国的到来》，伦敦：艾伦·莱恩出版社，2003 年；《当权的第三帝国（1933—1939）》，伦敦：艾伦·莱恩出版社，2005 年；《战争中的第三帝国（1939—1945）》，伦敦：艾伦·莱恩出版社，2008 年。
7. 理查德·J. 艾文斯：《大都会岛民：英国历史学家和欧洲大陆》，剑桥：剑桥大学出版社，2009 年。
8. 西奥多·S. 哈梅罗："内疚、赎罪与德国历史书写"，《美国历史评论》第 88 期，1983 年 2 月，第 65—70 页。
9. 理查德·J. 艾文斯："导言：威廉二世时期的德国和历史学家"，载理查德·J. 艾文斯：《威廉二世时期的德国社会与政治》，伦敦：克鲁姆·赫尔姆出版社，1978 年，第 11—39 页。
10. 哈梅罗："内疚、赎罪与德国历史书写"，第 70 页。
11. 艾文斯："导言：威廉二世时期的德国和历史学家"，第 22—23 页。
12. 艾文斯：《捍卫历史》，第 212 页。
13. 理查德·J. 艾文斯：《希特勒的阴影：西德历史学家和逃离纳粹历史的尝试》，伦敦：I. B. 陶里斯出版社，1989 年。
14. 理查德·J. 艾文斯：《为希特勒说谎：大屠杀、历史和大卫·欧文审判》，伦敦：沃索出版社，2001 年。
15. 参见 E. H. 卡尔：《历史是什么？》，理查德·艾文斯撰引言，贝辛斯托克：帕尔克雷夫出版社，40 周年版，2001 年。
16. 艾文斯：《捍卫历史》，第 179—181 页。
17. 参见 A. W. 珀杜："本周畅销书：《大都会岛民》"，《泰晤士高等教育》，2009 年 7 月 9 日，登录日期 2013 年 10 月 24 日，http://www.timeshighereducation.co.uk/407279.article。

第三部分：学术影响

9 最初反响

> 要点
>
> - 艾文斯的理论中受到最有力批评的，是他关于客观性和追求真相的观点——后现代主义者希望表明这些概念早已过时。
> - 《捍卫历史》的批评者既有传统的经验主义者，也有后现代主义者；艾文斯在回应批评时，指责他的批评者有政治动机，并表明了他们是如何误解了他的论点的。
> - 这是学者之间的一次重大论辩，个性冲突有时比哲学辩论显得更为突出。

批评

理查德·J.艾文斯的《捍卫历史》有意在传统经验主义历史观和后现代主义理论对历史学科有效性的挑战——对通过历史研究发现客观真理的可能性有着不同的理解——之间找到一条中间道路。他的著作受到了两大阵营的密切关注，尽管它基本上是受欢迎的。

一位具有较强政治动机的批评者是保守派历史学家尼尔·弗格森*。在弗格森看来，历史不需要捍卫，因为它在英国的教育机构中比以往任何时候都更受欢迎。弗格森坚称，这本书对那些具有"宽泛保守属性"的历史学家来说是"粗鲁的"。[1]艾文斯社会史研究的核心问题和方法是从他早期学术生涯中"新左派"的立场发展而来，似乎与弗格森宽泛的右翼立场水火不容。[2]

后现代主义者批评艾文斯拒绝以后现代主义哲学本身的术语展开讨论，以至于误解和曲解了他们的思想体系以及思想家个人。此外，许多人坚持认为，《捍卫历史》提倡一种过时的客观性概念，为保守的历史方法辩护，并提出自相矛盾的论点。尤为激烈的批评来自历史学家基思·詹金斯，而他也是艾文斯学术攻击的主要目标。在《为什么研究历史?》一书中，詹金斯用一章的篇幅阐述艾文斯的著作，指出他对历史的辩护是资产阶级保守思想的一部分，他的著作并非为了维护历史本身，而是为了维护艾文斯在"历史俱乐部"内的学术地位。[3]

艾文斯的著作招致的其他批评则比较多样化。例如，美国历史学家乔伊斯·阿普尔比认为，艾文斯的论点是完全没有必要的，所谓"后现代主义拒绝在历史实践中追求客观真理"是站不住脚的，不值得如此多的关注。[4] 以研究历史学理论而闻名的美国学者林恩·亨特*以其在历史理论方面的研究而闻名，她批评艾文斯不断地提及 G. R. 埃尔顿与 E. H. 卡尔之间过时的争论。[5] 以研究当代文学理论而闻名的学者安东尼·伊斯特霍普*指出艾文斯著作的最后一段来自卡尔《历史是什么?》的最后一段，以此作为依据，声称艾文斯的观点与经验主义客观性毫无二致。

> "这本书所引起的反应五花八门，且互相矛盾，这使我深感震惊。我真没想到一本书能让人以这么多不同的方式去阅读或误读。"
> ——理查德·J. 艾文斯:《捍卫历史》

回应

艾文斯在 1998 年至 1999 年期间通过伦敦历史研究所的网站详细回应了他的批评者，这些答复构成了《捍卫历史》自 2000 年以来版本中的《后记》的基础。

艾文斯颇具说服力地反驳了针对他著作的大多数批评。虽然他承认了伊斯特霍普所指出的一些史实错误，但他驳斥了其他批评家，并指责许多人误读了他的著作。据艾文斯说，詹金斯把本不属于他的观点强加于他身上（并错误地将所有历史学家都定性为同质的精英），还把他关于客观性的立场描述为传统的经验主义。[6]虽然艾文斯注意到19世纪德国历史学家利奥波德·冯·兰克某些研究方法的重要性，但在整本书中，他都主张一种有限的客观性，而其中历史学家的主观性作用是不可或缺的。[7]

以研究性别和巫术著称的后现代历史学家黛安·珀基斯*指责艾文斯持保守观点，并歪曲她的著作。[8]在谈到他对弗格森和珀基斯这样的历史学者的论述时，艾文斯指出，他只使用了作者自己的原话，并在他的书中做了不偏不倚的表述。他辩称，在整本书中，他显然赞成历史的多样性和多元性，包括一些后现代主义思想。该书的目的是维护历史书写实践与对过去的准确表述之间的联系，而不是维护任何特定的学派。

冲突与共识

艾文斯承认，他在讨论某个哲学家或理论家时犯了某种奇怪的"低级错误"。[9]但总的来说，他坚持自己的立场，并强调他的书以一种近乎"滑稽可笑"的方式被误读或误解。[10]艾文斯坚持认为，他那些后现代主义论敌变得"如此愤怒"，恰恰是因为他揭露了他们虚伪的政治姿态，并详细列举了他们对自己的论点进行歪曲和任意曲解的种种乖谬。[11]一些措词激怒了他们，如把后现代主义者描述为"智识领域的蛮族"，艾文斯在手稿中留下了这些词语，因为

"我相信没有人会愚蠢到如此程度",以至于照字面理解这些表达。[12] 如此怒气冲冲、冷嘲热讽的交流意味着,艾文斯和他的批评者之间几乎毫无和解的余地。

辩论经常触及个人谩骂和学术竞争,而不是澄清重要的哲学观点。以历史传记闻名的学者道格·门罗*在一篇总体上持肯定态度的评论文章中指出,虽然艾文斯振振有词地为自己辩护,使自己不受"坚持埃尔顿的国家历史或性别历史观点"的批评,但这些都与他对客观性的看法无关,客观性有时是不明确的。[13] 同样,艾文斯在因果关系上的立场也很薄弱,他对卡尔的许多观点的坚持也值得质疑。正如詹金斯所指出的,艾文斯没有回答因果关系在实践中如何起作用,以及如何能够正确选择一连串层级性的因。[14]

来自各方的广泛批评表明,人们对这一广受欢迎的著作还未达成共识。这也许是意料之中的事;《捍卫历史》旨在驳斥一些重要而又相互矛盾的思想流派,并提出艾文斯对那些个人著作的批判性分析。

---

1. 尼尔·弗格森:"历史已死,历史万岁!",《星期日泰晤士报》,1997年9月21日。
2. 理查德·J. 艾文斯:《捍卫历史》(第2版),伦敦:格兰塔出版社,2001年,第261页。
3. 基思·詹金斯:《为什么研究历史?伦理和后现代主义》,伦敦:劳特利奇出版社,1999年,第106—112页。
4. 乔伊斯·阿普尔比:"它真的需要捍卫吗?",《时代文学增刊》,1997年10月31日,第10页。

5. 林恩·亨特:"历史需要捍卫吗?",《历史研讨会期刊》第46卷,1998年12月,第241—249页。
6. 艾文斯:《捍卫历史》,第277—285页。
7. 艾文斯:《捍卫历史》,第271—272页。
8. 黛安·珀基斯:"对理查德·艾文斯的回应",《聚焦历史》,登录日期2013年10月24日,http://www.history.ac.uk/ihr/Focus/whatishistory/purkiss/.html。另见黛安·珀基斯:《历史中的女巫:早期现代和20世纪的表现》,伦敦:劳特利奇出版社,1996年。
9. 艾文斯:《捍卫历史》,第292页。
10. 艾文斯:《捍卫历史》"后记",第270页。
11. 艾文斯:《捍卫历史》"后记",第285页。
12. 艾文斯:《捍卫历史》,第296页。
13. 道格·门罗:"《捍卫历史》书评",《社会史期刊》第36卷,2002年第1期,第242—244页。
14. 詹金斯:"关于理查德·艾文斯",载《为什么研究历史?》,第105页。

10 后续争议

要点 🗝

- 一些人认为艾文斯的著作作出了很重要的贡献,但现在已成为明日黄花;一些人担心他的论点支持了对当代各种文化分析的理论方法的敌视态度。
- 艾文斯的史学史著述体现了一种大趋势,即在研究该学科发展的同时,还要审视其社会作用。
- 该书对历史学专业本科课程产生了巨大的影响;后现代主义理论的一些要素,如作者对风格的关注和自我反思(研究者在分析过程中的个人角色意识),在很大程度上已经被吸收进了历史学专业之中。

应用与问题

理查德·J.艾文斯的《捍卫历史》不仅仅是一部论辩历史的著作,而且还将这种论辩传播给了历史学专业及学术界内外的新受众。自出版以来,艾文斯的著作不断地被其他著作提及,如英国历史学家约翰·托什的《历史为什么重要?》(2008)和鲁德米拉·乔丹诺娃的《实践中的历史》(2006)为学生提供了关于各种史学论辩的有益介绍,[1] 只是他们的方法不那么具有争议性和论辩性,这是因为,与否认大屠杀这种热点问题相比,后现代主义的其他挑战似乎不那么紧迫。

托什和乔丹诺娃对理论方法持开放态度,并且希望与艾文斯在客观性问题上所表现出来的保守主义保持距离。托什在1999年的一篇书评中不屑一顾地评论说,艾文斯是在"靠近历史学正中心的某个地方"发表意见的,并支持"绝大多数"历史学家都可能赞同的论点。尽管托什深知,艾文斯之前一直享有处在"社会史最前沿"的盛誉,但仍然对后者著作中"令人惊讶的保守"结论感到失望。[2] 事实上,对于那些深信理论好处的历史学家来说,其主要担心是,艾文斯对经验主义的辩护实际上可能会使学生远离更加概念化的思维。正如历史学家 R. D. 安德森*在 2001 年所言:"总的来说,不需要警告英国学生防范理论泛滥;问题反倒是如何引起学生对经验主义之外的东西生出兴趣,如果认为艾文斯的书使反理论态度合理化,这就太遗憾了。"[3] 艾文斯认为极端相对主义及"客观性不可实现"这些相关理念是危险的,对此许多历史学家都会深表赞同,但他们也常怀戒心,以防《捍卫历史》被用作试图切断与其他学科对话的工具。

> "因此,与其他历史学新方法一样,后现代主义似乎更适合历史中的某些领域而不是全部领域。21 世纪的历史研究和写作应取后现代主义理论之长而用之,而上述思想认识,则是朝着该方向迈出的第一步。"
>
> ——理查德·J. 艾文斯:《捍卫历史》

思想流派

尽管《捍卫历史》很重要,特别是对于学生、教师和一些历史学家来说更是如此,但在过去几年中它对历史研究实践的影响力有所下降。该书中许多思想都可以追溯到其他历史学家,并且早已在主流史学思想中得到确立。但该书为现行的史学实践进行了全新的、直言不讳的辩护,并进一步提出了关于历史学家的公共角色和公共活跃性的重要问题。而该问题已经变得日益重要，这主要是由于历史节目在英国电视上流行，历史出版物具有商业吸引力，以及历史学家在课程改革方面发挥建言作用。随着《捍卫历史》的出版，相关著作陆续问世，开始反思历史学家如何把自己的研究传播给更广大的受众，以及如何把学术的影响拓展到对过去更宽泛的表述上。[4]

艾文斯对历史专业发展的概述，体现了他对过去30年史学史深深的迷恋。[5] 有时这种迷恋导致历史学家试图重振某些往昔历史学家的重要性。例如，历史学家大卫·康纳丁*向20世纪早期著名的英国历史学家G. M. 特里维廉致敬（尽管艾文斯怀疑这位怀旧的"贵族"作家将来会"继续被忽视"）。[6] 最近，迈克尔·本特利*展示了各种"现代主义"的方法，这些方法在20世纪初期振兴了英国的历史编纂学，唤起了对共同思维模式和风格技巧的关注。[7] 另外，这种迷恋也使人们更加意识到，历史叙事在现代世界可以通过不同的媒体进行交流——包括戏剧、电影、电视和广播——而正是这些叙事构成了文化记忆。[8] 作为英国最卓越，也是最有名气的历史学家之一，艾文斯阐述并评论了历史学家在公共生活中日益凸显的重要性。

当代研究

不论《捍卫历史》表达的诸多思想是已经过时还是处于最前沿，其都在历史学领域产生了重大影响，并为许多后续著作所引用。为反击后现代主义，该书为历史学学科整体——而不是某个具体的方法或研究话题——进行了全面的辩护。因此，该书涉及的范围可能过于宽泛，无法促使任何特定的学派形成。尽管如此，最近许多关于历史学方法的讨论都引用了它,其中包括2012年一篇关于档案使用的文章、2010年一篇讨论为历史调查进行各种辩护的文章以及2000年一篇关于历史、大屠杀和历史学的文章。[9]

  艾文斯反对后现代理论主义某些方面的观点,可能会让一些读者认为他全盘否定后现代主义思想。基思·詹金斯认为,虽然艾文斯似乎对后现代主义思想的某些要素持温和的态度,但这仅仅是一种策略,以掩饰他对后现代主义思想的反感。[10]然而与此相反,艾文斯坚持认为,采用后现代主义方法论的某些观点,同时拒绝接受其关于不可能获得真相的破坏性观点,这是大有裨益的。[11]艾文斯预言,后现代主义在这种程度上可以被调节和同化为"合法的次专业"。他将这一过程与摇滚乐进行了比较:摇滚乐始于年轻人的离经叛道,但之后却逐渐演变成一种音乐风格,其激进的棱角也被修剪掉了。[12]艾文斯的这一说法已得到事实证明。后现代主义研究已被纳入一些大学历史学系,正如后现代主义思想已融入历史学家的方法库中一样。

---

1. 约翰·托什:《历史为什么重要?》,贝辛斯托克:帕尔格雷夫·麦克米伦出版社,2008年;鲁德米拉·乔丹诺娃:《实践中的历史》(第2版),伦敦:霍德·阿诺德出版社,2006年。
2. 约翰·托什:"简要说明:捍卫历史",《英国历史评论》第114卷,1999年,第805页。
3. R. D. 安德森:"书评:《捍卫历史》",《苏格兰历史评论》第79卷,2000年,第106页。

4. 彼德·曼德勒:《历史与国家生活》,伦敦:侧影书局,2002年。
5. 约翰·伯罗:《史学史:从希罗多德到20世纪的史诗、编年史、传奇和调查》,伦敦:企鹅出版社,2009年。
6. 大卫·康纳汀和G. M. 特里威廉:《历史中的生命》,伦敦:丰塔纳出版社,1993年;理查德·J.艾文斯:《捍卫历史》(第2版),伦敦:格兰塔出版社,2001年,第163页。
7. 迈克尔·本特利:《英国历史的现代化:现代主义时代的英国历史编纂学(1870—1970)》,剑桥:剑桥大学出版社,2006年。
8. 拉斐尔·塞缪尔:《记忆的剧院:当代文化的过去和现在》第1卷,伦敦:沃索出版社,1996年。
9. 玛丽·林德曼:"外交档案的严谨性魅力",《德国历史:德国历史学会学报》第29卷,2011年第2期,第283—304页;亚历山大·里昂·麦克菲:"捍卫(我的)历史",《反思历史:理论与实践期刊》第14卷,2010年第2期,第209—227页;迈克尔·丁滕法斯:"真理的他者:伦理学,大屠杀历史和语言学转向后的史学理论",《历史与理论》第39卷,2000年第1期,第1—20页。
10. 基思·詹金斯:《为什么研究历史?伦理和后现代主义》,伦敦:劳特利奇出版社,1999年,第95—114页。
11. 艾文斯:《捍卫历史》,第156页。
12. 艾文斯:《捍卫历史》,第203页。

11 当代印迹

要点 🗝

- 尽管《捍卫历史》对于本科生来说仍然是一本介绍历史研究方法的重要参考书，但在今天看来，它并不包含多少开创性思想。
- 该书在21世纪初对抵制后现代主义发挥了重要作用，并引起了文化转向*。
- 艾文斯一直受到批评，因为他采取了论辩式的攻击手段——富有挑衅性的批评——而且未能与后现代主义哲学家充分展开论战。

地位

理查德·J.艾文斯的《捍卫历史》仍然被用于向大学生展示关于历史本质的争议。这是该书的中心目标，从这个意义上来讲，对该书的批评实际上提高了它的实用性。它进一步扩大了有关历史的一般性辩论，使更多的学生了解到客观性、因果关系以及历史研究如何进行实践等关键问题。然而，这些哲学问题被卷入了一场非常激烈的相互指责之中。一位评论者反映说，在《后记》中，艾文斯对批评他的人进行了冗长的反驳，他给人的印象是"脾气暴躁、脸皮薄"，表现出"敏感的防范性"，经常诉诸"令人厌恶的"人身攻击。[1]

虽然《捍卫历史》刚出版就备受关注，并且一直被视作一部关于历史本质的极具价值的著作，但在最近的时期里，对它的关注较少。也许毫不令人奇怪的是，后现代主义者基思·詹金斯和阿伦·芒斯洛*在2004年出版了由45位历史学家的著作选编而成的

《历史的本质读本》，他们决定将艾文斯排除在他们的选集之外。[2]而一些更为传统的历史学家认为《捍卫历史》过于宽泛，而且太缺乏独创性，以致无法作出决定性的贡献。约翰·托什在他2008年的著作《历史为什么重要？》中指出，艾文斯没有说明历史的社会依据，也没有提出如何将其与广大公众联系起来的建议。[3]《捍卫历史》关注的是维护现有的历史观念，而不是全面勾勒出一种新的历史实践。不过，艾文斯显然认为，历史学家可以在纠正有关大屠杀的谎言方面发挥社会作用，就像他在大屠杀否认者大卫·欧文败诉的诽谤案审判中所起的作用一样。

> "这本书的主要目标之一是激发辩论，而不是终结讨论（而这也根本不可能）。一些人抨击这本书未能直面那些主要后现代主义思想家，他们理直气壮地——当然也是画蛇添足地——指出，所涉问题不可能在几百页的篇幅内得到解决。因此，重要的是让辩论继续进行。"
> ——理查德·J.艾文斯：《捍卫历史》

互动

《捍卫历史》进而要求学术界内外的读者去考量那些认为"过去的真相无足轻重"的理论所造成的影响。例如，艾文斯质疑澳大利亚学者黛安·珀基斯的说法，即历史学家应该讲述犹太人在奥斯威辛集中营的经历，仅仅因为这些故事在道德上如此"感人"，但他写道："这些故事是否真实，真的不重要吗？"[4]艾文斯坚持认为，学术严谨性和历史方法在准确回忆个人经历的过去和痛苦方面起着重要的作用。

20世纪90年代初的"文化转向"似乎势不可挡，它将法国大陆哲学中的许多重要概念引入了主流历史书写。然而，在21世纪初开始出现抵制迹象，反对历史纯粹基于话语（由一系列假设和声明构成的"文本"）和陈述的极端历史观，其倡议者甚至包括林恩·亨特等前代人物。[5]

许多领域的历史学家都在寻求某种方式，将语言和话语与其生活的社会环境联系起来（艾文斯称之为"将语言和思想重新置于一个真正的历史语境里"），[6]这不一定意味着背离理论。相反，正如彼得·曼德勒*等著名的文化史学家所建议的那样，这意味着借鉴更广泛的理论，并以更批判和务实的方式加以利用。曼德勒认为，"文化史存在的问题"其中一部分就是历史学家忽视了各种文化形式的"延伸"。换言之，他们过于热衷描述各种话语，而没有花足够的时间研究为什么某些话语被相信，被哪些群体相信，而又有哪些话语不被相信。[7]

持续争议

后现代主义哲学的拥护者对艾文斯著作的回应，混杂了思想、个人和政治各种因素。争论的焦点是关于客观性概念的思想争论，而另外一些批评则似乎是基于个人的，即某些人为自己在《捍卫历史》中所受到的评价表示不满。这在一定程度上是由于艾文斯的论战风格。黛安·珀基斯称艾文斯对她的描述是"歇斯底里的"，并指责艾文斯就是一个"保守的辩论机器"。[8]

在其雄辩的《后记》中，艾文斯花较大篇幅对他的历史学家对手们进行详细的论辩，但很显然，他没有充分地讨论罗兰·巴特和雅克·德里达等思想家的贡献，尤其是他们关于语言和意义的理论。历史学家R. D.安德森为此抱憾地说，艾文斯"在整幅图片中留下了这么多的空白",尤其是没有抓住机会对法国社会理论家和历史学家米歇尔·福柯的著作进行建设性的探讨,福柯作为一名"疾病与犯罪历史学家",本该与艾文斯是最接近的。[9]

艾文斯著作中另一个严重的疏漏是反殖民和后殖民理论。然而,对历史学科的权威性攻击最尖锐的那些学者们,首先想要做的是重述那些附属群体的生活经历,其次是重新建构历史叙述的方式,给予殖民者和被殖民者以平等的声音。德里达的著作在这方面也有很大的影响力,结果就是文学评论家和历史学家受到解构主义的影响,把现存的历史学实践描述为"白色神话"。[10]

对于一些后殖民思想家(研究殖民主义的各种社会、历史和文学遗产的思想家们)来说,这意味着一种"使欧洲乡土化"的共同举措,以便找到一些书写历史的方式,使压迫性的西方等级制度不再重现。[11] 虽然《捍卫历史》有效地击退了后现代相对主义观念对客观性概念的挑战(后现代主义认为不可能通过历史研究得出任何客观"真相"的观点),但该书未能解决新的后殖民主义方法论对历史研究的批评和挑战。

---

1. 道格·门罗:"《捍卫历史》书评",《社会史杂志》第36卷,2002年第1期,第242页。
2. 基思·詹金斯和阿伦·芒斯洛:《历史的本质读本》,伦敦:劳特利奇出版社,2004年。
3. 约翰·托什:《历史为什么重要?》,贝辛斯托克:帕尔格雷夫·麦克米伦出版社,2008年,第18页。

4. 理查德·J. 艾文斯:《捍卫历史》(第 2 版),伦敦:格兰塔出版社,2001 年,第 242 页。
5. 林恩·亨特、维多利亚·邦内尔和理查德·别尔纳茨基编:《超越文化转向:社会与文化研究的新方向》,加利福尼亚州伯克利:加利福尼亚大学出版社,1999 年。
6. 艾文斯:《捍卫历史》,第 217 页。
7. 彼得·曼德勒:"文化史的问题,还是游戏时间结束了?",《文化与社会史》第 1 卷,2004 年第 1 期,第 94—117 页。
8. 黛安·珀基斯:"对理查德·艾文斯的回应",《聚焦历史》,登录日期 2013 年 10 月 24 日,http://www.history.ac.uk/ihr/Focus/whatishistory/purkiss1.html;另见艾文斯:《捍卫历史》,第 304 页,第 307 页。
9. R. D. 安德森:"书评:《捍卫历史》",《苏格兰历史评论》第 79 卷,2000 年,第 106 页。
10. 罗伯特·杨格:《白色神话:书写历史与西方》,伦敦:劳特利奇出版社,1990 年。
11. 迪佩什·查卡拉巴蒂:《地方化欧洲:后殖民思想和历史差异》,新泽西州普林斯顿:普林斯顿大学出版社,2000 年。

12 未来展望

要点

- 《捍卫历史》对于本科教学依然很重要，对于一般公众亦是如此，它表明为什么历史学家应该坚持对过去真相的追求。
- 该书虽然没有提出一种新的研究和书写历史的模式，但阐明了历史学实践和理论的多样性。
- 《捍卫历史》的影响力随着世界和全球历史的发展而逐渐减弱。

潜力

自从1997年理查德·J.艾文斯的《捍卫历史》一书出版以来，人们对后现代主义可能要为历史研究提供一个新范式（一种解决各种研究课题的总体知识框架）的担忧已经完全消退——尽管后现代主义某些思想仍可见于美国期刊《表述》和《历史与理论》上，因为荷兰历史哲学家弗兰克·安克斯密特是这些期刊的编委之一。甚至在文学界和哲学界，也出现了某种抵制，有学者反对将所有社会现象都描述成类似文学文本的偏执做法。正如艾文斯所指出的，这种类比没什么用，因为"大多数时候，绝大部分人既不是读者也不是作者。"[1] 除此之外，21世纪初，人文学科对物质性有了更深的认识，也就是说，思想家们一直在研究知识的物质的、触觉的及具象的形式，而这些形式不能被简化为纯粹的话语。[2]

在《捍卫历史》一书中，他也明确指出，维护真理、反对歪曲事实是历史学家的公共责任，这对德国而言具有特殊的相关性和敏感性。艾文斯的新书《历史和记忆中的第三帝国》（2015）阐述了这一主题，该书收集了他的新闻评论和书评，描绘了过去20年以来对纳粹主义解读的演变过程。艾文斯表明，学术中日益增长的"全球转向"*（转向撰写全球历史，将地理上分散的研究领域联系起来）促使后续研究转向将纳粹主义与欧洲其他形式的帝国建设进行比较，更具争议的是，将大屠杀与其他形式的种族灭绝相比较。艾文斯权衡了这种解读的好处和危险，其文集在总体上证明了艾文斯的信念，即历史学家有道德义务尽可能诚实和负责地描述过去。[3]

> "历史学家不仅解构了其他历史学家的叙述，也解构了对过去的叙述。"
>
> ——理查德·J. 艾文斯：《捍卫历史》

未来方向

《捍卫历史》描述了自20世纪60年代以来，历史学家的地理视野是如何迅速拓宽的。与G. R. 埃尔顿和休·特雷弗-罗珀等怀疑论者不同，一些历史学家不再把自己国家的历史或西方的历史放在优先地位，而是将目光投向更广泛的国际关联上来。艾文斯赞许地指出："由此，历史学不仅比以往更加兼收并蓄，在其内容和方法上，欧洲中心的色彩也愈来愈淡了。"[4]然而，正是这种扩展带来了新的问题。一方面，人们对帝国历史的兴趣日益高涨，但这并没有扭转英国学校里外语学习的衰退趋势。艾文斯在2009年发表《大都会岛民》时，因感到研究欧洲的学术传统现在似乎正在受到威胁，希望对之加以维护。[5]另一方面，关于历史方法的重大问题已从客观性和相对主义（后现代主义挑战的核心）转向考虑如何将全球不同地区多种多样的、往往是暴力的经历进行整合并给予公平对待。[6]

这种全球维度鼓励了对"大历史"的追求——"大历史"即倾向于考虑比传统历史叙述更长的时间跨度和更大的地理单元的一种趋势。颇具影响力的年鉴学派以其对社会史的研究方法而著称,以艾文斯本人对该学派的钦佩及其对以往粗疏的历史分期的蔑视,可能会让他对上述方法产生共鸣。[7]哈佛历史学家戴维·阿米蒂奇*是这种"大历史"方法最热情的提倡者,他与人合著了《历史宣言》(2014),旨在为历史学科制定一套新的规程。他的建议是重点关注具有针对性的大数据和大问题,以证明历史对政府决策来说是息息相关且大有意义的。[8]该书引起了极大的分歧,受到了广泛而尖刻的批评。[9]这也许提醒我们,任何一位学者在试图定义和表述一个在观点上变得如此多样化的历史专业时,都面临着种种困难。

小结

《捍卫历史》一书值得特别关注,它激情澎湃、简洁清晰而又妙趣横生,其目的是保护历史不受后现代主义挑战的影响。20世纪80年代和90年代,海登·怀特、弗兰克·安克斯米特和基思·詹金斯等学者把新的语言哲学应用于历史研究。在该书中,艾文斯概述了为什么历史仍然是一门有效的学科。尽管艾文斯承认,历史研究不能避免对当前急务的关切,也无法摆脱历史想象力的作用,但他坚持认为,历史学家所使用的文献可以让他们与过去的事件和人物建立直接的联系。艾文斯提出,的确可能获得某些有限的客观性,因为证据的本质约束了历史学家所能表达的东西。好的历史学家可以运用"诗意和想象力"来对历史材料提出质疑,而书面证据则使这一做法"受到事实的约束"。[10]

该书深受早期历史理论著作的影响,尤其是马克思主义历史学家 E. H. 卡尔的著作《历史是什么?》，其对"语言学转向"以及后现代主义挑战的讨论，为新一代人复苏了这些往昔的话题。然而，该书是对主流历史学实践的辩护，因此不算是革命性的著作。它之所以重要，是因为它讨论了后现代主义对历史学的目的、有效性和实践的质疑，为学生和教师提供了一个有效切入点来讨论这门学科。艾文斯写这本书的动机之一是要表明，后现代主义可以导致一种极端形式的相对主义，它容忍法西斯主义和种族主义思想，甚至否认大屠杀。这一警告直接源于艾文斯作为卓越的德国社会历史学家的地位。该书在历史学家之间就历史学专业的目的和规范等话题引发了广泛的（有时甚至针锋相对的）讨论，至今仍然具有重要意义。

---

1. 理查德·J.艾文斯:《捍卫历史》(第2版)，伦敦：格兰塔出版社，2001年，第186页。
2. 参见丹尼尔·米勒:《物质性》，北卡罗来纳州达勒姆：杜克大学出版社，2005年。
3. 理查德·J.艾文斯:《历史和记忆中的第三帝国》，纽约：小布朗出版社，2015年。
4. 艾文斯:《捍卫历史》，第181页。
5. 理查德·J.艾文斯:《大都会岛民：英国历史学家和欧洲大陆》，剑桥：剑桥大学出版社，2009年。
6. 迪佩什·查卡拉巴蒂:《使欧洲乡土化：后殖民思想和历史差异》，新泽西州普林斯顿：普林斯顿大学出版社，2000年。
7. 艾文斯:《捍卫历史》，第156页。
8. 戴维·阿米蒂奇和乔·古尔迪:《历史宣言》，剑桥：剑桥大学出版社，2014年。在线浏览：http://historymanifesto.cambridge.org/。
9. 彼得·曼德勒和黛博拉·科恩:"历史宣言：批判"，《美国历史评论》第120卷，2015年第2期，第530—542页。
10. 艾文斯:《捍卫历史》，第251页。

术语表

1. **年鉴学派**：以法国学术期刊《经济和社会史年鉴》命名的思想流派。年鉴学派史学家坚持历史写作应借鉴不同学科的目标和方法,并涵盖过去的社会、心理和经济。年鉴学派中的重要学者包括马克·布洛克、吕西安·费弗尔和费迪南德·布劳德尔。

2. **反犹太主义**：对犹太人的敌视或偏见。

3. **奥斯威辛**：一个集中灭绝营,位于纳粹占领的波兰,是大规模屠杀数百万欧洲犹太人的关键地点。

4. **冷战（1947—1991）**：第二次世界大战结束至1991年,美国和苏联之间的军事和意识形态紧张时期。这两个集团从未发生直接的军事冲突,而是进行秘密战争和代理人战争,并相互实行间谍活动。

5. **文化转向**：20世纪80年代至90年代初期流行的文化历史方法。文化转向形成的部分原因是将历史与文学批评、艺术史和社会人类学等邻近学科联系得更加紧密。

6. **解构主义**：始于20世纪60年代的文学理论运动,质疑意义与语言之间的联系。法国哲学家雅克·德里达断言,文本由于其各种可能性及不断变化的意义而变得不可穷尽。

7. **决定论**：历史学中的"决定论"指的是认为某些发展必然以某种特定的方式发生。决定论者忽视偶然性的作用,而强调某些历史趋势和事件是必然的、不可避免的。

8. **经验主义**：一种思想理论,认为通过仔细研究原始资料和证据就可以获知过去的真相。

9. **欧洲中心**：着眼于欧洲的观念、关注点、历史和文化;对国际事件的历史分析首先考虑其对欧洲的影响。

10. **女权主义**：一种政治运动,旨在通过确保妇女享有平等的政治、社会、经济和文化权利来理解和推翻两性之间持久的不平等状况。

11. **全球转向**：20世纪90年代和21世纪初书写全球历史、研究跨国历史和国际"连接性"历史的趋势。

12. **大萧条**：1929年美国股市崩盘后开始的全球经济衰退。

13. **史家之辩**：德语术语 *Historikerstreit*，可译为"历史学家之间的论争"。它发生于20世纪80年代的西德，当时包括迈克尔·斯蒂尔默和恩斯特·诺尔特在内的几位保守派历史学家希望消除多数德国人的"负罪感"，并改变大屠杀在历史上的特殊地位。

14. **历史编纂学**：研究历史书写或研究某一历史论辩随时间而发生的演变。

15. **历史工场**：20世纪60年代由英国历史学家拉斐尔·塞缪尔发起的一场运动，主张"自下而上看历史"，以普通人而不是精英的视角叙述历史。

16. **大屠杀**：二战期间纳粹德国有计划、有组织地驱逐和大规模消灭犹太人的行为。一些学者认为，大规模灭绝和迫害其他群体（如社会主义者、同性恋者、罗姆人和那些有精神疾病的人）的行为也应包括其中。

17. **语言学转向**：许多学科的发展开始关注语言和哲学的重要性。人们曾经把"语言学转向"与后结构主义的思想（特别是雅克·德里达的著作）联系在一起。

18. **马克思主义**：一系列包括历史学、社会学、经济学和政治学在内的多领域研究理论和方法。它是以19世纪中期卡尔·马克思的思想为基础的。马克思主义的思想内容非常丰富，其核心原则之一是相信历史的唯物主义发展、阶级结构和各种社会力量的辩证本质。20世纪中期英国的马克思主义史学家有埃里克·霍布斯鲍姆、克里斯托弗·希尔和E.P.汤普森。

19. **物质转向**：出现于20世纪90年代和21世纪初的一种思想学派。受考古学、艺术史和人类学学者的启发，其践行者希望鼓励学者更多地考虑对象和事物的非话语属性。

20. **元叙事**：一种叙事方法，旨在完整地或全面地描述历史的变化，并揭示历史必然是朝着某种进步的方向前进的。后现代主义者声称元叙事具有压迫性,或不再重要。

21. **纳粹德国**:指 1933 年至 1945 年间由阿道夫·希特勒领导的极端右翼的国家社会主义德国工人党(纳粹)在德国的统治时期。"纳粹主义"一词是纳粹党为政治运动和意识形态创造出来的。

22. **新左派**:在英美两国使用的术语,用于描述 20 世纪 60 年代末至 70 年代的一场运动。该运动希望实施广泛的社会改革,但反对传统的左翼和马克思主义政党的做法。

23. **客观性**:认为存在可以判断或观察的真实现象,而该现象独立于情感或个人偏见。

24. **后现代主义**:该术语被广泛用于多个学科,用来描述 20 世纪早期出现的一套理论体系。其理论之一认为,现实是人类思维的一种构念。后现代主义对普遍规律、普世价值或概念给予根本否定。在历史学上,后现代主义强调现在去表述过去是困难或不可能的,历史研究具有主观性本质,并重视语言在历史研究中发挥的作用。

25. **相对主义**:一组彼此相连的概念,认为不存在绝对的或普遍的真理、知识或道德,而这些思想与文化、历史环境或社会有着内在联系。

26. **社会史**:历史学的一个分支,强调要研究过去社会的所有群体,而不仅是政治精英;社会史学家通常致力于对不同社会阶层、生活条件和家庭关系进行研究。社会史深受马克思主义影响,在 20 世纪 60 年代和 70 年代得到迅速发展,但在 20 世纪 80 年代和 90 年代影响有所减弱。

27. **苏联**:一个存在于 1922 年至 1991 年间的"超级大国",主要以俄罗斯为核心,还包括东欧和亚洲北部。在冷战中,苏联代表共产主义阵营,而美国是其主要"对手"。

28. **目的论**:认为事物不可避免地朝着某个目标或目的运动;就历史而言,目的论的思维意味着存在一个推动社会发展的目的和总方向。

29. **第三帝国**:1933 年至 1945 年战败期间,由阿道夫·希特勒和纳粹党在德国建立的政权。它梦想能够像第一神圣罗马帝国那样存在一千年,结果只持续了 12 年。

30. 威廉二世德国：1871 年至 1918 年间，特别是 1888 年至 1918 年间由威廉二世皇帝统治的德国。

31. 第一次世界大战（1914—1918）：始于欧洲帝国之间的大规模冲突，但后来扩大到美国和大部分殖民国家，并以德国及其盟国的失败而告终。

32. 第二次世界大战（1939—1945）：全球性军事冲突，以同盟国（英国、法国、美国和苏联）击败轴心国（纳粹德国、法西斯意大利和日本帝国）而告终。

人名表

1. 大卫·亚伯拉罕，迈阿密大学法学教授。作为普林斯顿的一位年轻历史学家，他因 1981 年的著作《魏玛共和国的崩溃》受到了相当多的关注。这本书因其操纵证据来源、忽视反证的方式，以及采取了党派立场，声称大企业帮助纳粹掌权，而遭到了诸多批评。

2. R.D. 安德森，爱丁堡大学历史学教授，致力研究法国和苏格兰教育系统。

3. 乔伊斯·阿普尔比（1929 年生），美国历史学家，专门研究历史学以及美国共和国早期的政治和经济思想。

4. 弗兰克·安克斯米特（1945 年生），荷兰历史哲学家，目前任荷兰格罗宁根大学思想史和历史学理论教授。

5. 戴维·阿米蒂奇（1965 年生），哈佛大学思想史和国际史学者。2014 年他与乔·古尔迪合著了《历史宣言》并引发热议。

6. 罗兰·巴特（1915—1980），法国文学理论家、语言学家和哲学家。他为许多不同的理论作出了贡献，包括结构主义和后结构主义。

7. 凯瑟琳·贝尔西（1940 年生），文学评论家和德比大学客座教授，一直倡导创新理论和后现代理论方法。

8. 迈克尔·本特利（1948 年生）历史学家，专门研究英国维多利亚时代的政治和 20 世纪的思想文化。

9. 大卫·康纳丁（1950 年生），英国历史学家，专门研究 19 世纪和 20 世纪的英国历史，著有关于贵族、帝国和君主制的经典著作。他也是英国学校历史教学的主要顾问。

10. 简·卡普兰，历史学家，主要研究方向是纳粹德国，在美国和英国都担任过许多学术职务。

11. E. H. 卡尔（1892—1982），英国马克思主义历史学家，著有经典的两次世界大战期间的外交史和苏联史。他 1961 年的著作《历史是什么？》对理查德·J. 艾文斯产生了巨大的影响。

12. **斯特凡·科里尼**（1947 年生），英国文学评论家，剑桥大学思想史教授。他专门研究英国 19 世纪和 20 世纪的高雅文化。

13. **罗伯特·达恩顿**（1939 年生），美国历史学家，专门研究 18 世纪的法国和书籍史。理查德·J. 艾文斯对他的经典著作《对猫的大屠杀》（1984）进行了讨论，以说明一些后现代主义思想是如何影响文化史书写的。

14. **保罗·德曼**（1919—1983），出生于比利时的文学理论家，定居美国并在哈佛大学任教。作为一位重要的解构主义理论家，德曼在 20 世纪 80 年代被披露曾在二战期间为比利时的一家通敌报纸撰写了大量反犹太文章。在由此引发的争议中，德里达和他的批评者就德曼的哲学观点和政治行为之间的关系进行了相互指责。

15. **雅克·德里达**（1930—2004），出生于阿尔及利亚的法国哲学家，因发展了解构主义和后结构主义而闻名。德里达被引用（以及被误引）最多的话就是："文本之外一无所有。"

16. **安东尼·伊斯特霍普**（1939—1999），曼彻斯特城市大学英语研究教授，常常对那些著名的批评家进行打破常规的评论，并对大陆哲学和知识创新持开放态度。

17. **G. R. 埃尔顿**（1921—1994），出生于德国的英国历史学家，他专攻都铎时期的历史，认为 16 世纪 30 年代形成了中央集权政府和"政府革命"。他对马克思主义历史学家以及各种背离政治或国家历史的做法持强烈批评态度。

18. **尼尔·弗格森**（1964 年生），英国历史学家，以研究金融、国际化和帝国历史的著作而闻名。除了拥有自己的媒体生涯，他还是英国政府聘任的学校历史教学顾问。

19. **弗里茨·菲舍尔**（1908—1999），极具影响力的德国历史学家，以其研究第一次世界大战的开创性著作而闻名。

20. 米歇尔·福柯（1926—1984），法国哲学家，他写了关于认识论、话语、性行为和社会机构规训等的开创性著作。福柯无疑是二战以来最重要的思想家之一，而理查德·J.艾文斯在自己的书中却遗漏了他，真是令人震惊。

21. 托马斯·L.哈斯克尔（1939年生），美国历史学家，专攻美国史。他是休斯敦莱斯大学历史学塞缪尔·G.麦肯名誉教授。

22. 克里斯托弗·希尔（1912—2003），英国马克思主义历史学家，他专攻17世纪英国史，研究在英国内战期间活跃的民主派和持不同政见者等激进团体。

23. 格特鲁德·希梅尔法布（1922年生），美国历史学家，撰写了关于英国维多利亚时代思想文化的著作，并呼吁回归传统和保守的历史研究方法。

24. 林恩·亨特（1945年生），美国历史学家，以其关于法国大革命和历史理论的著作而闻名。同时她也是20世纪90年代初文化转向最著名的倡导者之一。

25. 大卫·欧文（1938年生），英国作家，因其关于第二次世界大战和纳粹德国的作品而声名狼藉。欧文作为所谓大屠杀"修正主义"领袖人物之一，于2006年在奥地利被捕入狱（在奥地利否认大屠杀是非法的）。

26. 基思·詹金斯（1943年生），英国后现代主义历史学家和历史哲学家。詹金斯在《为什么研究历史？伦理与后现代主义》中回应了理查德·J.艾文斯的批评。

27. 鲁德米拉·乔丹诺娃（1949年生），英国历史学家，现任达勒姆大学教授。她撰写了关于历史上的性别和医学的著作，以及一部关于历史实践本质和视觉文化应用的著作。

28. 黛博拉·利普施塔特（1947年生），美国历史学家，以其研究大屠

杀的著作而闻名。目前她是亚特兰大埃默里大学的杜罗特教授，专门研究现代犹太人以及大屠杀。

29. 彼得·曼德勒（1958年生），剑桥大学历史学教授，同时也是19世纪和20世纪英国文化史方面的专家。他的著作内容广泛，主要研究现代英国对文化遗产的开发以及历史与社会科学的关系。

30. 道格·门罗，新西兰昆士兰大学兼职教授，从事历史传记和20世纪太平洋的研究工作。

31. 阿伦·芒斯洛（1947年生），斯塔福德郡大学历史学教授，被公认为后现代主义和解构主义方法的先驱。

32. 彼得·诺维克（1934—2012），美国历史学家，以其历史理论方面的著作而闻名。

33. 黛安·珀基斯（1961年生），澳大利亚历史学家，撰写了关于性别与文学、巫术以及英国内战的著作。

34. 利奥波德·冯·兰克（1795—1886），柏林大学德国历史学家，他为基于史料的批评奠定了基础，因此被视为这一学科之父。他对现代欧洲的宗教史和外交史进行了广泛的研究。

35. 琼·沃勒克·斯科特（1941年生），美国普林斯顿大学历史学家。她发表了大量关于法国社会史和文化史的文章，是性别和女权主义历史研究领域最重要的思想家之一。

36. 约瑟夫·斯大林（1878—1953），苏联领袖。他自1928年起一直担任共产党总书记，直至1953年去世。

37. 劳伦斯·斯通（1919—1999），英国近代早期历史学家，在牛津大学和普林斯顿任教。理查德·J.艾文斯引用了他与休·特雷弗-罗珀因一篇文章而引发的众所周知的冲突。在那篇文章中，斯通声称，英国内战前夕，贵族的经济力量在衰落。特雷弗-罗珀通过揭露斯通对史料的滥用和误读，而将他彻底驳倒。

38. 基思·托马斯（1933年生），英国历史学家，1986年至2000年在牛津大学担任现代史教授。作为借用人类学方法的先驱，托马斯在其著作中研究了近代英国早期的魔法、迷信、宗教和关于自然的思想。

39. **修昔底德**（公元前460—公元前395），希腊最伟大的历史学家之一，其著作叙述了雅典和斯巴达之间毁灭性的伯罗奔尼撒战争。

40. **约翰·托什**，英国历史学家，目前任罗汉普顿大学历史学教授。他关于历史中的男性主义和历史本质的著作颇受关注。

41. **G. M. 特里维廉**（1876—1962），英国历史学家，以其关于17世纪至19世纪英国政治的著作和他对辉格党/自由党思想的拥护而闻名。他也是社会史领域的先驱，不过理查德·J. 艾文斯对他的文学和贵族风格不屑一顾。

42. **休·特雷弗-罗珀**（1914—2003），牛津大学近代历史学钦定讲座教授。他是近代早期英国和欧洲史的专家，也是第三帝国的早期研究者，但在20世纪80年代他确认为真的"希特勒日记"后被证明为伪造，这使其名声受损。

43. **海登·V. 怀特**（1928年生），美国历史学家，他出版了许多与文学批评相关的历史理论著作。他主张所有的历史书写都要采用一种叙事"情节化"形式。

44. **娜塔莉·泽蒙-戴维斯**（1928年生），出生于加拿大的早期近代欧洲历史学家，她以在妇女史、历史学与人类学之间的界限以及小说和故事在历史档案中的地位等方面的开创性研究而闻名。

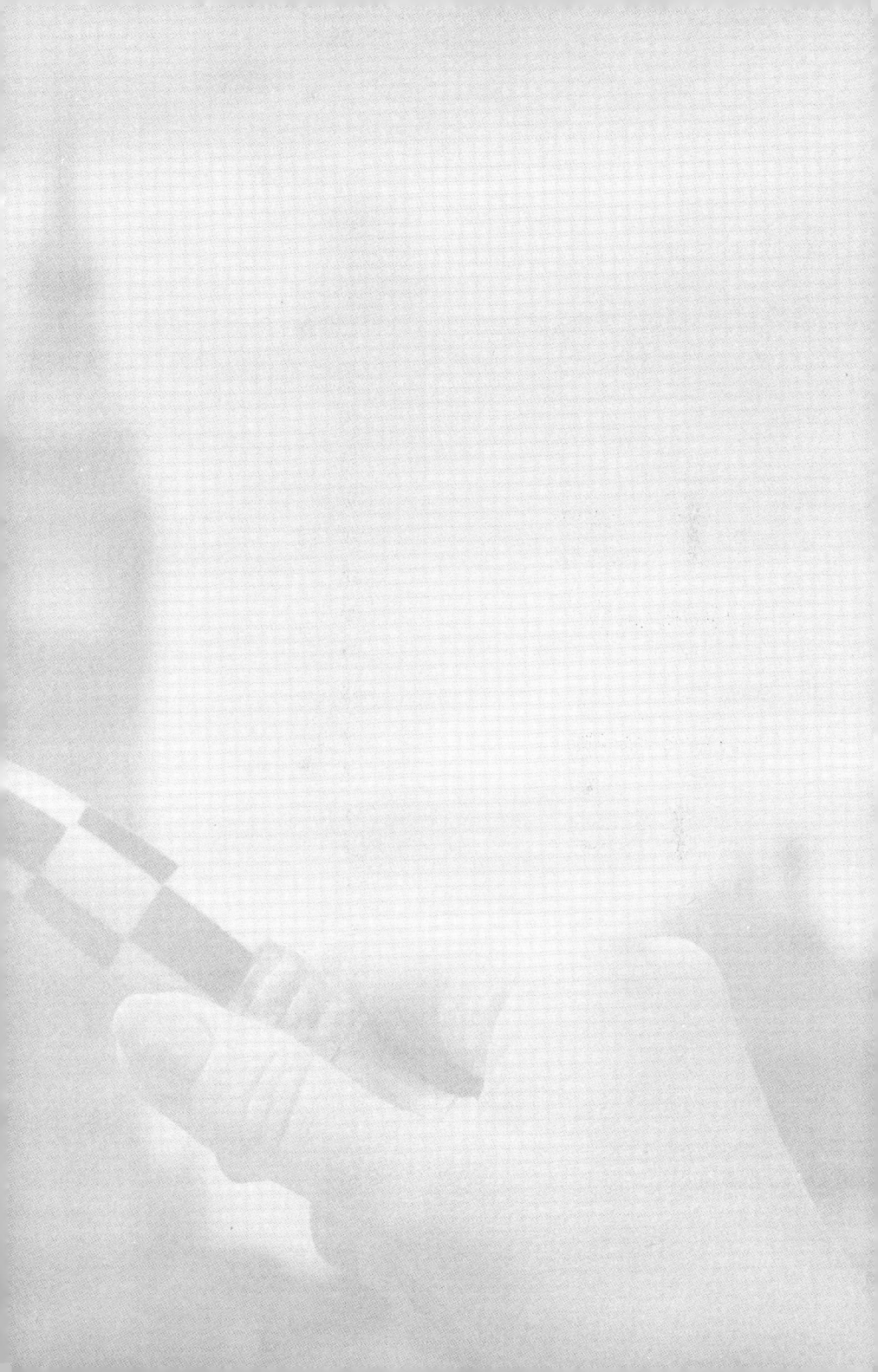

WAYS IN TO THE TEXT

KEY POINTS

- Richard J. Evans is a British historian, born in 1947, famed for his work on imperial and Nazi Germany,* and his writings on historical method (that is, methods of research and analysis in the academic field of history).
- Written in the context of the mistrust of "objective* truths" and traditional Western historical methods typical of postmodernist* beliefs, *In Defence of History* (1997) offers a robust defense of the pursuit of accuracy and neutrality in the process of researching, writing, and studying history.
- In this work of historiography*—roughly, the study of the methods and aims of historians—Evans charts the development of history as a scholarly practice; employing examples from his own research, he demonstrates that history still has a distinct place among the social sciences.

Who Is Richard J. Evans?

Richard J. Evans, the author of *In Defence of History* (1997), is one of the foremost historians of Germany working in Britain today. Born in the north-east London suburb of Woodford in 1947, he studied history at Oxford University with some of the greatest historians of the time, and developed an interest in historical methodology. He was particularly drawn to the historian E. H. Carr's* seminal work *What Is History?*, a text whose influence is clearly evident in his own writing. Evans decided to specialize in German social history,* inspired by the controversy around Fritz Fischer,* a historian who held Germany responsible for the outbreak of World War I.* Holding lectureships at Stirling

University, the University of East Anglia, and Birkbeck College (University of London), Evans published highly acclaimed studies on German feminism,* criminal justice, and public health.

While teaching at Birkbeck, Evans decided to publish *In Defence of History*, alarmed at the growth and implications of postmodern approaches to analysis within the historical profession; postmodernism is a movement relevant to contemporary arts and cultural analysis, usually characterized by a disbelief in objectivity and the sense that all interpretations are equally valid. As a historian concentrating on modern Germany, Evans recognized the potential danger in this framework. While he had previously written specifically on German historians wrestling with the Third Reich* (the regime created by Adolf Hitler and the Nazi Party in 1933 that lasted until the end of World War II* in 1945), *In Defence of History* was the first time Evans addressed broader questions of historical method.

His expertise on Nazism led to his appointment as a witness in the Irving*–Lipstadt* libel case, in which the British author David Irving unsuccessfully sued the American historian Deborah Lipstadt for libel; Evans's testimony was pivotal in exposing Irving as a denier of the Holocaust* (the industrial extermination of many millions of European Jewish people by Nazi Germany during World War II).

In 2008 Evans was appointed as Regius Professor of History at the University of Cambridge and used his inaugural lecture to champion the tradition of previous British historians who had written about continental Europe (published as *Cosmopolitan*

Islanders in 2005). Author of an acclaimed recent trilogy charting the rise and demise of the Third Reich, Evans has been awarded numerous honors, including the presidency of Wolfson College, Cambridge, and a knighthood from the Queen in 2012.

What Does *In Defence of History* Say?

In Defence of History is Evans's attempt to confront the dangers posed by postmodern theory to the practice of history.

The debate about whether history could ever be a science with identifiable laws and the ability to predict future outcomes, and whether it could lay claim to objectivity—the belief that it is possible to identify "real" phenomena regardless of personal prejudices—was not new. Indeed, Evans was keenly interested in how this question had been debated in the 1960s by the British historians G. R. Elton* and E. H. Carr. But the existing skepticism about historical method had been placed on a new footing due to the impact of emerging ideas about language, sometimes referred to as the linguistic turn* in critical theory, articulated by literary critics and philosophers such as the French thinkers Roland Barthes* and Jacques Derrida.*

These theorists suggested that the meanings of words are not fixed to the objects or ideas to which they refer but, rather, that they function through their difference from, and relation to, words and other signifiers—such as sounds and images—that point us towards meaning. Historical events, then, could not be seen to have a single, fixed meaning or single interpretation. Building on these insights, thinkers and academics such as the historian and cultural critic

Hayden White* suggested that historical writing was not radically dissimilar to literature, since different historians could examine the same piece of evidence and draw different conclusions and interpretations. The British postmodern historian Keith Jenkins* went further and argued that documentary records are necessarily incomplete and never really impartial, making it impossible for historians to use documents in order to gain access to the "truth" about the past.

This observation struck at the heart of history as a discipline—throwing into doubt its methods, its purpose, and its intentions to tell the truth.

Evans aimed to refute the postmodern challenge on multiple fronts. First, by re-describing the development of the historical discipline, he showed that debates around objectivity, selection of source material, and politics of representation were not new; history as a discipline had often been more diverse, more self-critical, and more radical than its postmodern enemies liked to purport. Second, he maintained that postmodernists' claims about texts and language were internally inconsistent on a conceptual level, and threatened to delegitimize their own practice (that is, that postmodern assumptions were not secure in themselves, and might jeopardize the very ability of historians to work toward sound analysis). Third, Evans argued that postmodern skepticism toward the possibility of objectivity carried unexpected social and political consequences. He recognized that if there were no standard for judging truth or accuracy, this opened the door to a variety of distorted or reactionary ideas, including Holocaust denial.

It is important to note that the primary focus of his attack was not postmodern philosophers, but those historians who had cited these ideas in an attempt to overhaul how history was written.

Evans's fundamental strategy for refuting the postmodernists' position on truth, causation, and objectivity involved grounding his counterarguments in practical examples rather than abstract linguistic theory. His defense of the pursuit of objectivity was welcomed at a time when many academic historians feared that postmodernism threatened to completely undermine the idea of shared methods and rules of evidence within the discipline. Although both orthodox and postmodern commentators criticized it, the book was a commercial success; 12 editions have been published to date, and it has been translated into several European and Asian languages. The history of its reception reveals a great deal about the ongoing development of how and why historical research is conducted.

In Defence of History remains an ideal introduction to the methodological controversies—that is, disputes concerning the ways in which historical research and analysis is conducted—that raged in the field at the end of the twentieth century.

Why Does *In Defence of History* Matter?

While the work is not revolutionary in its thought, what sets *In Defence of History* apart is its ability to provoke thought about how history is practiced, and the way in which it informs readers about a broad range of thinkers and historians, from traditional empiricists* (that is, those who believe in the authority of knowledge founded on evidence that can be verified by observation) to postmodernists. The work maps the evolution of the discipline since the 1960s to encompass many types of social history (that is, roughly, historical studies that focus on all sections of society). Evans also draws on his personal research into modern German history to illustrate his own approach. His ability to discuss complex and wide-ranging issues in a simple and engaging manner makes his means of expression almost as important as the ideas contained within the work, countering the opaqueness of postmodern theory with a grounded, approachable rhetorical style. His commitment to objectivity does not restrain him from providing an often very subjective, critical account of his peers; *In Defence of History* also offers a showcase of lively, even notably forceful, argument.

In addition, Evans's public profile, and his numerous appearances as an expert on issues of historical memory and the legacy of Nazism, demonstrate the relevance of his approach far beyond the academic world. Evans's involvement in the Irving–Lipstadt trial highlighted the grave importance of producing an accurate and verifiable version of past events. In his subsequent writings he has reflected further on the public and civic function of historians, showing how scholarship can inform popular understandings of the past.

While questions remain about the way Evans conceives objectivity, subjectivity (that is, interpretation influenced by personal feelings or assumptions), and causation in history, *In Defence of History* has, as the reviews indicate, provoked and widened debate. The substantial and combative Afterword that accompanies the editions from 2000 onward shows how many vital questions of method and of ethics were raised by Evans's intervention. The fundamental issue at stake is the question of whether an objective historical truth is desirable or even conceivable. Evans succeeded in arguing convincingly that, while subjectivity will surely play a role in historians' interpretations, objectivity remains worth pursuing.

SECTION 1
INFLUENCES

MODULE 1
THE AUTHOR AND THE HISTORICAL CONTEXT

KEY POINTS

* *In Defence of History* remains one of the most influential and lucid accounts of historical method to appear in the past generation.
* Evans had emerged as an esteemed social historian,* allowing him to comment authoritatively on recent historical trends.
* Evans was writing against the backdrop of the breakdown of classic Marxist* interpretations—that is, interpretations founded on the analytical methods of the political theorist and economist Karl Marx—and new pressures on the institutions of higher education.

Why Read This Text?

Based on a series of lectures, Richard J. Evans's *In Defence of History* was published in September 1997. The title reflects a justifiable anxiety arising from the intellectual landscape in the late 1980s and early 1990s; in particular, it attempts to defend the practice of history from what Evans sees as the threat of extreme postmodernism* (a movement in the arts and cultural analysis that has questioned long-established assumptions in fields such as literature and the social sciences) and the challenge that postmodern ideas pose to concepts of scholarly objectivity,* the neutrality of facts, and the scientific nature of history.

In the work, Evans attempts to demonstrate the vitality of

history as a means for accessing the past, while also defending the importance of rigorous historical methods. Evans notes that in the mid-1990s, academic history had seen a serious challenge from postmodern thinkers, including the historians Keith Jenkins* and Hayden White* and the philosopher of history Frank Ankersmit.*

Evans provided a concise and influential account of how historical methods had evolved. He argued that historians were indeed capable of finding out the "truth" about what happened in the past, even if this truth was always partial and provisional. Evans stirred up a great deal of controversy—so much so that *In Defence of History* prompted widespread reflection about what, if anything, historians could learn from postmodernism.

> "In this sense, the problem of how historians approach the acquisition of knowledge about the past, and whether they can ever wholly succeed in this enterprise, symbolizes the much bigger problem of how far society can ever attain the kind of objective certainty about the great issues of our time that can serve as a reliable basis for taking vital decisions for our future in the twenty-first century."
> —— Richard J. Evans, *In Defence of History*

Author's Life

Richard J. Evans is a career historian. He was born in Woodford, a suburb of London, in 1947, the son of a teacher at a nearby school.[1] His parents had migrated to London from a small Welsh village during the early twentieth-century economic downturn known as the Great Depression.*[2] Evans went to study Modern History at

Jesus College, Oxford, in 1966. While studying at Oxford, Evans came into contact with the ideas of English Marxist historians (historians following the analytical assumptions of the political theorist and economist Karl Marx), the *Annales* school* (a deeply influential school of historians associated with the study of sections of society beyond men and women of high status), and the radical group involved with the *History Workshop* Journal* (a circle of historians who shared something of the aims and methods of both the Marxist and the *Annales* historians).[3] He attended lectures by noted historians Christopher Hill,* Keith Thomas,* and Hugh Trevor–Roper.* In 1969, Evans graduated with a first-class honors degree before moving to St Antony's College, Oxford, to complete his doctoral degree with research on the feminist* movement in Germany in the early twentieth century.

Following his studies, Evans held lectureships at the University of Stirling and the University of East Anglia. Between 1989 and 1998, Evans was professor of history at Birkbeck College, University of London, where he wrote *In Defence of History*, published in 1997. He was Regius Professor of Modern History at the University of Cambridge from 2008 to 2014.

Politically, Evans can be considered to be broadly center-left and was influenced by Marxist and left-wing ideas during his time at university.

Evans is best known for his works on Nazi Germany* and the Holocaust,* including his *Third Reich Trilogy*[4] and his study of postwar German historiography* *In Hitler's Shadow*.[5] In 2000, Evans was involved as an expert witness for the defense in a legal case brought by the British author David Irving* against the American historian Deborah Lipstadt,* who had named Irving as a Holocaust denier.[6] This experience demonstrates the practical importance of Evans's stance on truth and objectivity in historical analysis, one which insists that not all interpretations are equally valid—as the specific case of Holocaust denial clearly shows—and that historical evidence can be deployed to establish the facts of an event.

Author's Background

The late twentieth century saw a dynamic debate about the role of history in contemporary academia, with some scholars even proposing the wholesale dissolution of history as a discipline. During the 1980s and 1990s, a strand of postmodernism criticized traditional ideas about the authority of knowledge, particularly the prominence of the Western point of view, going as far as to advocate a *relativist** position, in which it is impossible for any historian to establish a single, objective "truth" about the past.

Although these views were uncommon among practicing historians, radical skepticism flourished among theorists of history and historiography. Drawing on French thinkers such as the literary theorist Roland Barthes,* the social theorist Michel Foucault,* and the philosopher Jacques Derrida,* the 1980s and 1990s saw a marked advance of critical theory within the humanities, accompanied by the political and ideological shift occurring at the end of the Cold War* (the long period of tension between the United States and its allies and the communist Soviet Union* and its allies, which began following World War II* and ended in the last decade of the twentieth century).

At the same time, many of postmodernism's defining features, such as a mistrust of grand narratives that purport to offer universal truths about the world, displaced the primacy of Marxism, an analytical method and political position that had previously provided the governing framework for many social historians.

This intellectual shift was linked to a wider realignment in higher education. Although history departments—and the total number of practicing historians—expanded rapidly in the 1960s and 1970s, this trend was reversed in the 1980s when right-wing governments came to power in Britain and the United States and cut funding to universities. This setback saw academic historians suffer a drop in their pay, independence, and status, and—according to Evans—the profession threatened to fragment into many disparate fields.[7] In their rejection of the idea of objective truth, postmodernists claimed that historians tended to propagate versions of the past that suited the needs and reflected the values of those in power and neglected the perspectives of marginalized people. Evans strongly disagreed with the more extreme, totalizing views of postmodernists towards history as a discipline, but he did acknowledge that the debate about how history is researched, written, and taught had distinct merit and value in 1990s Britain.[8]

---

1. Information on Richard J. Evans's career can be found via his personal website, http://www.richardjevans.com.

2. Daniel Snowman, "Daniel Snowman Meets the Historian of Germany, Defender of History and Expert Witness in the Irving Trial," *History Today* 54 (2004): 45.
3. Richard J. Evans, "Review: *The Annales School: An Intellectual History* by André Burguière," *London Review of Books* 31, no. 23 (2009): 12–14.
4. Richard J. Evans, *The Coming of the Third Reich* (London: Allen Lane, 2003); *The Third Reich in Power, 1933–1939* (London: Allen Lane, 2005); *The Third Reich at War 1939–1945* (London: Allen Lane, 2008).
5. Richard J. Evans, *In Hitler's Shadow: West German Historians and the Attempt to Escape from the Nazi Past* (New York: Pantheon Books, 1989).
6. Debra Lipstadt, *History on Trial: My Day in Court with David Irving* (New York: HarperPerennial, 2006).
7. Richard J. Evans, *In Defence of History*, 2nd ed. (London: Granta, 2001), 171–3.
8. Evans, *In Defence of History*, 179, 205.

MODULE 2
ACADEMIC CONTEXT

KEY POINTS

* Historical theory and historiography* (the study of the aims and methods of historians) both consider the evolution of the discipline of history.
* Conservative "positivist" historians tended to argue that historians can reconstruct the past accurately through studying documents; by contrast, those influenced by the intellectual current of postmodernist* thought denied that objective knowledge of the past was possible since all historians interpret their sources through the lens of their own cultural preoccupations, assumptions, and biases.
* Richard J. Evans tried to steer a course between the two, arguing that although a degree of subjectivity (roughly, the impossibility of conducting analysis without bias) on the part of historians is inevitable, documentary evidence can provide verifiable facts that helpfully constrain interpretations of past events.

The Work in Its Context

Richard J. Evans's *In Defence of History* was aimed primarily at those postmodernist thinkers who had questioned the relevance of history as a discipline through a fundamental challenge to notions of authoritative readings of past events and the concept of objectivity.* In the early nineteenth century, history had been placed on a more rigorous, scientific footing thanks to the teachings of the German historian Leopold von Ranke.* Ranke insisted that through scrupulous examination and comparison of archival materials, historians would be able to view the past "as it really was." Ranke and his supporters generally believed in the primacy of political and diplomatic history, and devoted their studies to understanding the behavior and decisions of statesmen.[1] A significant number of nineteenth-and twentieth-century scholars, however, believed that historians should pay as much attention to social groups beyond the ruling elite, to economic patterns, and the wider canvas of cultural life.

Some of the issues raised by the intellectual movement of postmodernism—such as the distorting role of the historian, or the unreliability of narrative—may have seemed novel but are actually many centuries old. "Two and a half thousand years ago," Evans observes, "the Greek historian Thucydides* complained in the preface to his history of the Peloponnesian War that poets and others were purveying false and imaginary accounts of what had happened, and announced his intention of setting the record straight."[2] The postmodern challenge in the 1980s was distinct, though, because its attack on historical objectivity—roughly, the possibility of arriving at "truth" in historical analysis—was linked to new theories of language. Many postmodernist thinkers insisted that words (or "signifiers") derive their meaning from their relation to, and difference from, other words rather than through a fixed relation to objects and concepts in the world. Influenced by French thinkers like Roland Barthes* and Michel Foucault,* postmodernists argued furthermore that meaning is generated by the reader; what the reader finds in a text, then, is far more important than the author's intention.

They argue that truth can never be absolute or universal, but is always partial or contingent (that is, dependent on certain assumptions or perspectives), and historical documents—like any other texts—are open to infinite interpretations. Evans wrote *In Defence of History* to show the danger of such views for historians.

> "The theory of history is too important a matter to be left to theoreticians. Practicing historians may not have a God-given monopoly of pronouncing sensibly on such matters, but they surely have as much right to try and think about them as anyone else; and the experience of actually doing historical research ought to mean that they have something to contribute which those who have not shared this experience cannot offer."
> —— Richard J. Evans, *In Defence of History*

Overview of the Field

Evans took the unusual step of beginning *In Defence of History* with reference not to recent postmodern thinkers but to the debates of an earlier generation. The German British historian G. R. Elton* and the British Marxist historian E. H. Carr* had outlined radically different views of historical method in the 1960s, with Elton endorsing the unmediated authority of historical documents, and Carr rejecting empiricism*—the idea that arguments should be founded on evidence certified by observation, and not through theory—in favor of history that recognized the interplay between archival evidence and present-day preoccupations. Despite their differences in outlook, Evans clearly admired both men. Unlike the postmodern historian Keith Jenkins,* who wrote about historical method in the abstract, Carr and Elton had honed their philosophical insights out of the experience of working with archives and documents.

We can broadly divide the scholars who write on questions of historical method into three groups. The first could be seen as a traditional, yet shrinking, group of empiricists like Elton. They believed in the possibility of reaching objective knowledge about the past through immersion in historical documents. The second group could be considered a broad majority of historians, including Carr and Evans, who believed, to different extents, that access to the past through historical research was possible but that this would always be fragmented, incomplete, and informed by the contemporary concerns of the historian. A third, newer group of theorists, the postmodernists, which included the Dutch historian Frank Ankersmit* and Jenkins, broadly believed that history could not provide an objective, disinterested account of past realities. For the postmodernists, historical writing is a construct of the dominant group in the present.

Academic Influences

In Defence of History was directly modeled on E. H. Carr's classic 1961 volume *What Is History?* Evans borrowed many of his chapter headings from Carr, and the last paragraph of the book is a "parody of Carr's final paragraph."[3] Carr's main influence on Evans's historiographical thinking was his assertion that history is a dialogue between past and present. It is not constructed solely from documentary evidence, nor entirely from the agenda of the historian, but arises from the interplay between the two. Carr also wanted to broaden the remit of historical research beyond the elite classes and world leaders. Yet Evans also offers a critique of an element of hypocritical selectivity in Carr's work, stating that Carr was "absolutely clear that those who had (in his view) contributed little or nothing to the creation of historical change as he saw it, such as women, or the pre-literate and politically unorganized masses, were not really deserving of the historian's attention."[4]

In addition, Evans was concerned about the teleological* assumptions in Carr's thinking (that is, his assumptions that history can be thought of as a procession of events towards a specific end). Carr thought the only developments worth writing about were those that succeeded in disrupting the present or changing the future. Evans recognized that such thinking had "extremely disturbing" implications, since it could lead the historian to turn away from telling the story of defeated causes or marginalized groups.[5]

In the same way, Evans did not agree with all of Carr's rather determinist* understanding of causation (that his, his idea that certain events were inevitable, given the prevailing circumstances), his support for models imported from the social sciences, or his belief in historians' powers of prediction.[6] While an admirer of Carr, Evans also strives to demonstrate the ways in which he is different from his predecessor.

1. Richard J. Evans, *In Defence of History*, 2nd ed. (London, Granta, 2001), 16–19.
2. Evans, *In Defence of History*, 260.
3. Evans, *In Defence of History*, 269.
4. Evans, *In Defence of History*, 212.
5. Evans, *In Defence of History*, 269–70.
6. Evans, *In Defence of History*, 138, 73.

MODULE 3
THE PROBLEM

KEY POINTS

- In the late twentieth century, practicing historians and critical theorists—roughly, thinkers working in the intersection of philosophy, literature, and the social sciences—questioned how well history could provide an objective and true account of the past, and whether this was possible at all.
- Postmodern* literary critics believed that texts could refer only to other texts; transferring this principle to history, postmodern thinkers such as the historians Hayden White* and Keith Jenkins* claimed that that historical writing only referred to the historian and the present.
- Evans retold the history of the discipline using examples from his own historical practice in order to make a case for the continuing value of history and of the pursuit of objectivity in writing about the past.

Core Question

Richard J. Evans's *In Defence of History* engages with fundamental questions about subjectivity—the impossibility of conducting historical analysis without influence from the historian's social context and personal biases. To what extent can history be considered objective* and true? How connected is the practice of writing about history to the object of its study, the past? In essence, these questions explore whether historians are capable of capturing and representing what actually occurred, or whether they are engaged in an exercise that reveals much more about their own present-day imagination and cultural context than past events.This issue is crucial to the validity of history as a field of study and research discipline. If, as some postmodernists suggest, the past is irrecoverable, then the concept of history as a study of the past becomes impossible and the discipline in its current form is finished. The idea of objectivity, truth, and accuracy are fundamental concepts for historians, and *In Defence of History* sets out to uphold the claim that historians can and should seek the truth about the past, even if this truth is only ever partial.

While these debates were a prominent aspect of the rise of postmodern thinking in the late twentieth century, such issues were not entirely new. As Evans observes, the possibility of a scientific or objective history was central to the formation of the discipline in the nineteenth century. In the 1960s, the empiricist* historian G. R. Elton* and the relatively radical Marxist* historian E. H. Carr* clashed over competing visions of how historians worked and what they could know. The answers given by Carr and Elton could not hold up when, in the 1980s, new forms of postmodern theory emerged and became fashionable within new philosophies of history and historiography.*

Informed by the "linguistic turn"* in philosophy and critical theory, which emphasized the role of language in all forms of cultural analysis, postmodernists challenged the basic premise of historical documents as transparent or referring to objective, external phenomena; rather, they suggested that history was inherently subjective, constructed in the mind of the historian and reflecting historians' cultural contexts. Postmodernist ideas did encourage a broader and more inclusive approach to presenting and interacting with historical evidence, which Evans duly acknowledges.[1] But he felt obliged to write *In Defence of History* in order to combat what he saw as some of postmodern philosophy's more dangerous possible implications, such as a disregard for rigor, blatant partisanship by the author, and moral relativism* (roughly, the position that moral judgment is not really possible since we cannot truly be certain of anything in matters of morals).

> "For present reality can be felt and experienced by our senses; but the past no longer exists, it is not 'real' in the same sense as the world around us in the present is real. It too has become a text."
>
> —— Richard J. Evans, *In Defence of History*

The Participants

The intellectual origins of the postmodern challenge to history can be seen in the literary criticism that appeared from the late 1960s. In France, theorists of language such as Roland Barthes* and Jacques Derrida* undermined conventional ideas about language and meaning. In Barthes's essay "Death of the Author" (1977), he dismissed the idea that readers can fully decipher or recover an author's original intention. For Barthes, meaning is secured through the act of reading and interpretation and not established definitively by authorial intention.[2] Barthes also noted that conventional historians believed that the past was waiting to be discovered, while Barthes viewed historical narratives as an "effect" created by literary and scholarly strategies.[3]

Similarly, the intellectual movement known as deconstruction* emphasizes the theory that our knowledge of the world is entirely mediated by language. As Derrida and other deconstructionists assert, meaning emerges out of the interplay between linguistic signs; therefore nothing can be imagined to exist "outside the text" and the reader's interpretation, not the author's intention, is the place where meaning is ultimately generated.[4]

These ideas were expanded upon and applied to history by the historians Hayden White, Frank Ankersmit,* and Keith Jenkins. Hayden White noted that history is a construct, like all literature, and is governed by a similar reliance on narrative. For White, within the confines of the historical method there are multiple, equally viable, ways of representing the past.[5] Jenkins observed that history is a discourse—that is, very roughly, a system of statements and assumptions making up a "text"—situated within a particular ideology; rather than attempt to study the past, Jenkins contended that historians should only study what other historians have said.[6] Like White, Ankersmit proposed that history is a construct, and the differences between historical works cannot be explained by research but by style.[7] Rather than study the past itself, history should focus on how the past is represented in the present.

These postmodern ideas fundamentally question the purpose and validity of history. *In Defence of History* is an attempt to rehabilitate the notion that historical texts are fundamentally connected to reality and that the principles of rigorous research, impartiality, and objectivity are still worth pursing for the practicing historian.

The Contemporary Debate

Evans resented the dismissive comments made about historians by postmodern thinkers, particularly those whose own publications displayed very little use of rigorous historical method. To refute their indictments, Evans drew extensively on the ideas of his predecessors, including an examination of the clash between Elton and Carr in the 1960s, going as far back as the British historian G. M. Trevelyan,* who was a pioneering practitioner of social history* in the late nineteenth and early twentieth centuries.

In Defence of History seeks to rebut the postmodern notion of history as essentially defunct by providing a more persuasive account of how the historical profession developed in the nineteenth and twentieth centuries. His demonstration of the range of topics covered and approaches used by historians convincingly undercuts the attempt by postmodernists to caricature historians as a single group with an elitist agenda. Using a balance of light wit and assertive argument, Evans cites debates on the techniques of nineteenth-century historians to debunk the supposed novelty of several postmodernist recommendations, such as the demand for historians to pay more attention to oppressed groups: "When a postmodern historian argues in the mid-1990s for a 'rediscovery of history's losers', one wonders what planet he has been living on for the last 30 years."[8] In tackling complex philosophical notions like objectivity, Evans drew on contemporary American debates featuring historians such as Peter Novick* and Thomas Haskell* regarding the subtle difference between objectivity and neutrality. Evans approaches the central concept of objectivity by providing numerous examples of historical theory and highlighting famous controversies among scholars—for instance the 1950s dispute between the British historians Lawrence Stone* and Hugh Trevor–Roper* over Stone's interpretation of documentary evidence regarding the status of the seventeenth-century English aristocracy, and the 1980s debate over the controversial link drawn by the American historian David Abraham* between big business and the rise of Hitler.[9]

1. Richard J. Evans, *In Defence of History*, 2nd ed. (London, Granta, 2001), 248.
2. Roland Barthes, "The Death of the Author," in *Image, Music, Text* (London: Fontana, 1977), 142–8.
3. Evans, *In Defence of History*, 94.
4. Jacques Derrida, *Of Grammatology*, trans. Gayatri Chakravorty Spivak (Baltimore, MD, and London: Johns Hopkins University Press, 1997); and Evans, *In Defence of History*, 94–5.
5. Hayden White, *Metahistory: The Historical Imagination in Nineteenth-Century Europe* (Baltimore, MD, and London: Johns Hopkins University Press, 1975); and Evans, *In Defence of History*, 100–1.
6. Keith Jenkins, *On "What Is History?" From Carr and Elton to Rorty and White* (London: Routledge, 1995); and Evans, *In Defence of History*, 97.
7. F.R. Ankersmit, *Historical Representation* (Stanford, CA: Stanford University Press, 2002).
8. Evans, *In Defence of History*, 213.
9. Evans, *In Defence of History*, 116–23.

MODULE 4
THE AUTHOR'S CONTRIBUTION

KEY POINTS

• Evans was inventive in addressing head-on the postmodern* challenge that objectivity* in historical research was impossible by showing through historical practice that some form of objectivity was desirable and possible.

• Evans attacked the political pretensions of postmodernism, by drawing on his own previous work on the Holocaust.*

• He offered an inclusive overview of the profession and showed the benefits and dangers of postmodernism.

Author's Aims

Richard J. Evans's *In Defence of History* engages directly with the criticisms coming from postmodernist thought. While some practicing historians thought that these arguments were not worth rebutting, Evans felt that this was complacent, in light of how influential such arguments were in undergraduate courses. Evans states unequivocally that the "theory of history is too important to be left to the theoreticians"[1] and sets out to persuade his readers "that it [is] possible to defend history as an intellectual undertaking by genuinely confronting and arguing with the extreme skeptics rather than by simply ignoring them or covering them with abuse."[2]

In his argument against extreme postmodernist views, Evans attempts to demonstrate inherent contradictions within postmodern concepts as well as the dangers of adhering to an extreme relativism,* a position in which any version of the past is a valid as any other.

Readers who expect a detailed dismantling of postmodern philosophy may also misunderstand the book's aims. While Evans wishes to counter extreme postmodern theory, he only does so in relation to the practice of history and not by making bigger philosophical interventions. One aim of *In Defence of History* was to narrate the phases through which the historical profession had developed, from the primacy of political history, through to the expansion of economic, social, and cultural history in the 1960s and 1970s. In doing so, Evans showed that historians were much more self-conscious about their own approach than their critics alleged. To illustrate this point he drew on examples from his own research. For instance, to respond to the postmodernist historian Hayden White's* argument that history is essentially a literary form, Evans relates how his own major book *Death in Hamburg* had been organized around "twelve parallel narratives" for "aesthetic" reasons, in order to present the material in "the most exciting and the most interesting way" while also being based in rigorous examination of historical fact.[3] For Evans, it is simply untrue that historians are naive, or unwilling to reflect on their active role in constructing stories about the past.

> *"Yet drawing up the disciplinary drawbridge has never been a good idea for historians ... Historians should approach the invading horde of semioticians, poststructuralists, New Historicists, Foucauldians, Lacanians and the rest with more discrimination. Some of them might prove more friendly, or more useful, than they seem at first sight."*
> — -Richard J. Evans, *In Defence of History*

Approach

Evans connected to specific social and political outcomes the philosophical question about whether objectivity was possible for historians. He rejected the claim made by the British postmodernist historian Keith Jenkins* that historians are simply involved in reproducing dominant values through institutions, particularly the university. He does this by documenting many instances of historians—especially those in social history*—who had explicitly set out to reveal injustices in the past and document the plight of oppressed groups, such as the working classes, women, and sexual minorities.[4]

Meta-narratives* of historical change—that is, roughly, accounts offering very broad perspectives on historical currents, suggesting that history is moving in a certain direction—are by no means inherently reactionary (that is, opposed to social progress), as he argues by reference to Marxism* and feminism* (the activism and theory of those advocating equality between the sexes). By extension he also questioned whether postmodernism was really as progressive and radical as it liked to pretend. Finally, Evans asks: if postmodernism alleges there are no objective grounds for deciding between different versions of history, beyond moral or aesthetic preference, then does it "give a license to anyone who wants to suppress, distort or cover up the past?"[5]

The force of Evans's critique came from his background in German history. During the 1980s a fierce dispute known as the *Historikerstreit** ("historians' quarrel") saw historians clash over the uniqueness of the Holocaust, by comparison with the policies of mass murder in other regimes, and the difficulties of reconstructing or morally understanding Nazi* crimes. Evans was a close observer of this debate, and in an article in the *Journal of Modern History* he set out his belief that social history could play a useful role in gaining a moral understanding about this period.[6] The debate made clear to Evans the stakes of the discussion about objectivity—and the dangers of insinuating, like some postmodernists did, that any version of the past was as good as any other.

Contribution in Context

In Defence of History, like E. H. Carr's* *What Is History?*, originated as a series of lectures given by the author.[7] Evans notes that he developed his ideas on historical knowledge, objectivity, and truth during his time at the British institution Birkbeck College in the 1990s. His arguments belong to the historical mainstream, and are close in many respects to other important writers on historical practice in the 1990s, such as the British historians John Tosh* and Ludmilla Jordanova.* Evans is careful to establish that he is not writing in defense of any one school, but, rather, championing a diversity of approaches to the past. Against those traditionalists such as G. R. Elton* or the American historian Gertrude Himmelfarb,* who had linked the defense of objectivity with a call for a return to elitist political history, Evans celebrates the widening of topics tackled by historians since the 1960s and 1970s. Evans's commitment to shared methods of verification accompanies a call for "a little intellectual tolerance" for the many different kinds of historical research.[8]

Unlike traditionalists such as Elton, who were hostile to social history, Evans sees many positive elements in the contemporary developments. New opportunities for trade and exchange were creating an "international marketplace of ideas" and a boom in interest in world history.[9] Evans's account of postmodernism is by no means entirely negative; its emphasis on the importance of narrative and style, for instance, has helped "reinstate good writing as a legitimate historical practice," as seen in the imaginative work of cultural historians such as Robert Darnton* and Natalie Zemon-Davis,* author of the bestselling *The Return of Martin Guerre*, in the 1980s.[10] Evans welcomes elements of postmodern thinking that were already compatible with long-running historical self-scrutiny, or could be beneficially assimilated into historical practice. *In Defence of History* is aimed at demolishing the more destructive elements of postmodernism, which threatened to explode any concept of truth in history.

---

1. Richard J. Evans, *In Defence of History*, 2nd ed. (London: Granta, 2001), 14.
2. Evans, *In Defence of History*, 255.
3. Evans, *In Defence of History*, 146.
4. Evans, *In Defence of History*, 20–68.
5. Evans, *In Defence of History*, 232–3.
6. Richard J. Evans, "The New Nationalism and the Old History: Perspectives on the West German *Historikerstreit*," *The Journal of Modern History* 59, no. 4 (1987): 761–97.
7. Daniel Snowman, "Daniel Snowman Meets the Historian of Germany, Defender of History and Expert Witness in the Irving Trial," *History Today* 54 (2004): 47.
8. Evans, *In Defence of History*, 182.
9. Evans, *In Defence of History*, 177.
10. Evans, *In Defence of History*, 244.

SECTION 2
IDEAS

MODULE 5
MAIN IDEAS

KEY POINTS

- Evans's primary aim is to defend an idea of weak objectivity* in historical practice, presenting history as a "weak" rather than "hard" science.
- Historical method is a crucial means for establishing what really happened in the past; while historians can never establish the truth of the past absolutely, they can approximate it through examining documents with professional rigor.
- Evans wrote in a deliberately clear and entertaining way, in order to contrast with the jargon used by his postmodern* enemies and to connect with a general reader.

Key Themes

In the introduction to *In Defence of History*, Richard J. Evans outlines the debate concerning the current state of the discipline and notes that some extreme postmodernists have questioned the validity of history and its future as a field of study. Here, Evans indicates that the central purpose of the book is to defend history from such criticisms and make the case for saving it. He does this through reviewing the evolution that the discipline has undergone in modern times.

While recognizing the importance of the nineteenth-century historian Leopold von Ranke,* an early champion of analytical archival research, Evans charts how notions of objectivity developed as historians began to favor an expanding variety of source material such as diplomatic dispatches, government minutes, and statistical records.[1] A social historian* by background, Evans welcomed the widening of the historical agenda in the 1960s to include documentary evidence from overlooked and excluded groups, combining the values of Ranke with the aims of progressive politics and a global history perspective.[2] *In Defence of History* is strongly grounded in Evans's commitment to thinking historically about the practice of history itself. He alleges that one of the weaknesses of postmodern historians is their unwillingness to engage in the "self-reflectivity" about their own position that they recommend to others, showing that one of the key faults of the postmodern critique of history is that the relativism* it espouses can easily be used to undermine its own position.[3]

Evans answers the claim that the inherent subjectivity of history prevents it from ever being scientific by asserting that that history is a "weak" science, unlike hard sciences such as physics, chemistry, and biology—areas of study governed by precise laws which permit a high degree of predictability in experimental settings. Elaborating on his interpretation, Evans insists that it is "always a mistake for a historian to try and predict the future. Life, unlike science, is simply too full of surprises."[4] While history is not based on laws that would allow historians to reliably predict the future, it has standards, methods, and a body of knowledge that make its practice scientific. It also produces generalizations about the past that can be tested. Evans outlines that history is a mix of science, art, and craft.[5] He shows that at their best, historians do not simply reproduce society's dominant ideas but have the power, through a commitment to rigor and accuracy, to, "punctur[e] the clichés of popular historical myth."⁶ When practiced fairly and thoroughly, history allows us to approach the truth of what happened in the past, even if this truth will always be approximate—"tenable though always less than final."⁷

> *"The language of historical documents is never transparent, and historians have long been aware that they cannot simply gaze through it to the historical reality behind. Historians know, historians have always known, that we can only see the past 'through a glass, darkly'. It did not take the advent of postmodernism to point this out. What postmodernism has done is to push such familiar arguments about transparency or opacity of historical texts and sources out to a set of binary opposites and polarized extremes."*
>
> —— Richard J. Evans, *In Defence of History*

Exploring the Ideas

Evans believes that some form of objectivity is possible because documents are connected to the reality of the past, and by comparing and examining them, historians can decipher which sources are reliable and illuminating. Document-based historical practice places limitations on what historians can realistically say about past events, and Evans believes postmodern theorists are wrong to insinuate that historians are free to invent or construct what happened. He also concedes, however, that historians will bring their own ideas to their research and cannot be totally independent of their cultural context. He echoes the Marxist* historian E. H. Carr* in claiming that historians "do not just listen to the evidence, they engage in a dialogue with it, actively interrogating it and bringing to bear on it theories and ideas formulated in the present."[8] With this core concept, Evans maintains that history is a valid discipline with persistent relevance.[9]

In making his points, Evans draws heavily on issues arising out of historical practice, grounding his assertions on these concrete examples rather than abstract theorizing. In reviewing the debate between G. R. Elton* and E. H. Carr on the subject of methods of research and analysis, he connects their philosophical outlook with their historical research. Elton advanced an empiricist* claim that historical documents, and the facts they contain, would speak for themselves; Evans exposes a blind spot in Elton's historical practice, suggesting that his unwillingness to consider the role of present-day context leaves a number of his own biases unacknowledged. A key example of this is the preference for strong government in the period of British history known as the Tudor era (1485–1603), which Evans believe reflects Elton's contemporary concerns.[10] Conversely, Carr believed that the historian's job was to look back from the vantage point of the present to identify what factors and events had contributed most to the progress of humanity. His own Marxist beliefs led him to equate "objectivity" with writing in defense of the progressive cause of the Soviet Union.*

While there are benefits to the transparent acknowledgment of a scholar's own political position, there is a danger that it can over-determine the historian's treatment of their subject matter—

that is, it can bear too much influence. In Evans's view, Carr's left-wing politics made his historical writing intolerant to any groups who had opposed the Russian Revolution of 1917, in the course of which the Tsar, the nation's ruler, was overthrown and a communist government was imposed.[11] These examples demonstrate how Evans sought to move beyond older, flawed definitions of objectivity while answering the postmodern challenge by showing what lessons can be learned from studying historical practice.

For Evans, an objective historian is both imaginative but confined by the limits of the evidence available for examination, while also resisting the intrusion of his or her own political or moral stance. While histories of the past will only ever be provisional, incomplete, and guided by external theories from the present, objectivity lies in the suspension of historians' own moral or political agenda in the selection and analysis of their source material.[12]

Language and Expression

Evans's work is lucidly written and engages with a wide range of sources and ideas. Because the text emerged from courses he taught at Birkbeck College in London, it was intended to serve as an introduction to major issues in the discipline, such as facts, causation, and objectivity in as clear and accessible a manner as possible.[13] Beyond the desire to achieve maximum accessibility and transparency, his writing style represents a strategy to highlight the difference between himself and the postmodernists who, in his view, "have developed a new level of specialized language and jargon, borrowed largely from literary theory, which has rendered their work opaque to anyone except other postmodernists." Evans seized on the obscure and inaccessible writing of the postmodernists as proof of their "narcissism" and "elitism."[14]

While welcoming the postmodernist attentiveness to how words are used, Evans recommends that historians "stick to a plain style unless they are very sure of what they are doing," since every point they make should be in the "service of clarification rather than obfuscation."[15] Evans takes pleasure in showing up the clumsiness or confusion that results from historians misusing language. Indeed one of the pleasures of Evans's prose comes from the cruel humor with which Evans pounces on his targets. The book is often irreverent towards some of the great names in the history of the profession, including Hugh Trevor-Roper* (citing his offensive comments about the "unrewarding gyrations of barbarous tribes" in Africa) and the early twentieth-century historian G. M. Trevelyan* (noting his "paternalistic and condescending stance towards [people of low social status] in history").[16] Evans is particularly unforgiving in showing up the sloppiness of his postmodern critics. For instance, in replying to the criticisms of the American historian Joyce Appleby,* he observes that "it is symptomatic of her scholarly standards that she even managed to misquote the book's title."[17] Such frank and biting asides help make the book a compelling read.

1. Richard J. Evans, *In Defence of History*, 2nd ed. (London: Granta, 2001), 110–11.
2. Evans, *In Defence of History*, 196–8.
3. Evans, *In Defence of History*, 115.
4. Evans, *In Defence of History*, 62.
5. Evans, *In Defence of History*, 66.
6. Evans, *In Defence of History*, 207.
7. Evans, *In Defence of History*, 253.
8. Evans, *In Defence of History*, 230.
9. Evans, *In Defence of History*, 73.
10. Evans, *In Defence of History*, 230–1.
11. Evans, *In Defence of History*, 226–8.
12. Evans, *In Defence of History*, 239.
13. Evans, *In Defence of History*, 257.
14. Evans, *In Defence of History*, 200.
15. Evans, *In Defence of History*, 69.
16. Evans, *In Defence of History*, 163, 178.
17. Evans, *In Defence of History*, 256.

MODULE 6
SECONDARY IDEAS

KEY POINTS

- Evans claimed that the intellectual movement of postmodernism* has brought some benefits to the writing of history but points out the dangers of exaggerating the role of individuals and personal subjectivities (that is, roughly, biases brought about by personal beliefs and historical context, for example).
- The continuing expansion and diversification of historical research threatened to undermine the idea of history as a single discipline—but Evans was optimistic about the continuing relevance of common standards.
- For Evans, postmodern thought is more applicable to some periods and problems than to others.

Other Ideas

Richard J. Evans's *In Defence of History* is particularly concerned with the implications of postmodernism for social history.* The influence of the "linguistic turn"*—an increased focus in many areas of cultural analysis on the importance of language to the understanding of "truth"—has brought greater prominence and visibility to marginalized groups within mainstream historical writing. As a social historian whose early research interests centered on the experiences of women and criminals in nineteenth-century Germany, Evans welcomed this aspect of postmodernist influence on historical practice.[1] Like the postmodernists, he deplored the insularity and Eurocentric* arrogance of an earlier generation of scholars[2] (that is, the narrow-mindedness and the assumption that historical research was founded on European perspectives). He also recognized that postmodernism had helpfully emphasized the importance of ordinary individuals in history. He cited the dictum of the influential nineteenth-century political theorist Karl Marx that "people make their own history, but they do not do it under circumstances of their own choosing."[3]

But while postmodernism had certainly helped social history develop, nuancing some of the clumsy older Marxist* models, Evans pointed out its potential for misuse. Its insights could be "pushed too far," leading to a situation where "we get an intellectual reductionism instead of a socio-economic one."[4] In other words, he thought postmodernism threatened to make the role of individual interpretation beyond reproach, neglecting the role of a wider social context and shared cultural truth.

A related danger came from the excessive importance attached to issues of personal identity. Postmodern historians were far too willing to speak as "I," openly invoking their own experiences and perceptions in describing the past, and valorizing the central role of empathy.[5] "The ultimate implication indeed is that no one can know anything beyond their own bodily identity. Experience is the sole arbiter of truth."[6] For Evans such a view was dangerous, since it suggested that only women could write the feminist* history, or only French historians should write the history of France. This position was unsatisfactory, since it deprived the oppressed of the opportunity tell the story of their oppressors, and disguised the extent to which writing good history means engaging with the "obviously other" as well as "the seemingly familiar."[7]

> "To search for a truly 'scientific' history is to pursue a mirage. Insofar as it has succeeded in generating new methods and techniques, this quest has of course been enormously beneficial ... History is not only a science in the weak sense of the word, it is, or can be, an art, in the sense that in skillful hands it can be presented in a literary form and language that achieves comparability with other literary works and is widely recognized as such."
> —— Richard J. Evans, *In Defence of History*

Exploring the Ideas

In order to demonstrate his view that postmodernists have presented a caricature of historians, Evans provides his own account of the state of the discipline. He shows how the profession has expanded massively since the 1960s, with the foundation of many new university departments. This expansion accompanied the fashion for social history and led to growing attention to groups and individuals who had previously been overlooked by mainstream historians.[8] This was a marked advance on the models of social history espoused by an older generation of historians. For instance, E. H. Carr,* despite his own work on the Russian Revolution, still suggested that the masses were only important enough to merit attention in historical writing when they were politically organized and advancing the cause of progress.[9]

Such narrow attitudes had now been overturned, and there had been a flourishing in women's history, black history, gay history, microhistory, and cultural history. Evans welcomes this democratization within historical thought. "Virtually everything of meaning or importance to contemporary humanity now has a written history and that means everything of importance to all kinds of people, not just to a small educated élite of the educated and powerful."[10]

Still, this expansion was not without its hazards. The initial hopes that social history could provide an overarching form of "total history" collapsed, as a host of subfields and subspecialisms developed. If each subfield had its own research questions and priorities, it became harder and harder to believe that there was a single historical discipline. Peter Novick,* a scholar noted for his theory of history, felt that history had fragmented so much that there was no longer a single scholarly community with its own norms and purposes.[11] Evans, however, was more optimistic. Electronic communication and frequent flights had made it easier for scholars from different parts of the world to share ideas. Moreover, although the theories historians used had diverged, this made it all the more important that they upheld common ways of referencing and presenting evidence. Contrary to the doubts of postmodernists, Evans insists, "interpretations really can be tested and confirmed by an appeal to the evidence ... it really is possible to prove that one side is right and the other is wrong."[12]

Overlooked

Evans deploys his expertise on German social history to show the serious consequences of viewing all interpretations as equally valid. Following a discussion of how postmodernity can be used to justify Holocaust* denial, Evans suggests that, like other new approaches to history, postmodernist theory may be more applicable to some areas of history than others.[13] Evans believes that theories that ignore the concept of the truth in relation to the Holocaust trivialize Nazism* and its victims. He quotes Jane Caplan,* principally a scholar of Germany's Nazi history, who claimed that postmodernism cannot be used so cavalierly when it is a question of the recent suffering and deaths of many people.[14] Although Evans suggests that it is inappropriate to use postmodern theory to consider the Holocaust, he does not ask the wider question: do certain theories or methods of history fit better with particular historical periods or historical events?

It is a question that has important implications. If postmodernist theory is not appropriate for discussing the Holocaust, are there other periods or subjects to which postmodernist ideas cannot be applied? If so, what criteria can we use to establish this, and to which other theories or historical periods is this applicable? Does this just relate to the sources available to the researcher, or to the morality of the event in question?

This subtle conceptual point, however, was lost amidst those critics who felt more angered at how their comments on historiography* had been associated with Holocaust denial. In Evans's defense, his reference to Holocaust denial was predictable in light of the controversy in the 1980s surrounding the rediscovery of the wartime anti-Semitism* of the Belgian literary critic Paul de Man,* a controversy that exposed the "exculpatory implications" of his deconstructionist* theories[15] (that is, it exposed the possibility that his anti-Jewish sentiments might have informed his theoretical arguments, since it was possible to use his theory to question the "truth" of documented, and terrible, historical events).

1. Richard J. Evans, *The Feminist Movement in Germany 1894–1933* (London: Sage Publications, 1976); *Rituals of Retribution: Capital Punishment in Germany 1600–1987* (Oxford: Oxford University Press, 1996).
2. Richard J. Evans, *In Defence of History*, 2nd ed. (London, Granta, 2001), 178.
3. Evans, *In Defence of History*, 189.
4. Evans, *In Defence of History*, 186.
5. Evans, *In Defence of History*, 200.
6. Evans, *In Defence of History*, 211.
7. Evans, *In Defence of History*, 214.
8. Evans, *In Defence of History*, 162, 171.
9. Evans, *In Defence of History*, 164.
10. Evans, *In Defence of History*, 165.
11. Evans, *In Defence of History*, 176.
12. Evans, *In Defence of History*, 128.
13. Evans, *In Defence of History*, 243.
14. Evans, *In Defence of History*, 242–3.
15. Evans, *In Defence of History*, 234.

MODULE 7
ACHIEVEMENT

KEY POINTS

* Evans succeeded in advancing a case for the importance of history and the pursuit of objectivity;* *In Defence of History* reached a large audience and was a commercial success in many countries.
* The book was also met with fierce criticism from adherents of postmodernism.*
* Evans's writing style is clear and engaging, and grounded in examples of history in practice.

Assessing the Argument

Richard J. Evans's *In Defence of History* largely accomplishes its aims. While the text has received much criticism from both traditional and postmodern thinkers for its content, Evans succeeds in outlining a personal view of why history is a valid field and why it should be defended; this work has become a standard historiographical* text for undergraduate students in many universities, particularly in the United States and the United Kingdom. Issued in hardback in 1997 and paperback in 1998, the book was quickly translated into Italian, German, Swedish, Turkish, Japanese, and Korean. Reviewers broadly agree that this work is comprehensive and convincing, but it is also a text about methodology that is surprisingly entertaining, not least because of the author's skill in skewering his opponents. As the journal *Kirkus Reviews* noted, Evans "brings colleagues, quick or dead, left or right, north or south, into the ring and merrily wrestles many to the ground."¹

In the 2000 edition, Evans claims that "stimulating debate was one of the book's principal aims," and in this, too, he was certainly successful.² In Evans's recollection, the sheer amount of coverage the book received was extraordinary, arousing "far more comment than I expected."³ Challenges to Evans's methods and conclusions came from so many quarters and ideological positions that he spent several years replying to them individually through the Institute of Historical Research online forum before answering the criticisms in print by publishing the Afterword to the 2000 edition.

> *"It is right and proper that postmodernist theorists and critics should force historians to rethink the categories and assumptions with which they work, and to justify the manner in which they practice their discipline. But postmodernism is itself one group of theories among many, and as contestable as all the rest. For my own part, I remain optimistic that objective historical knowledge is both desirable and attainable."*
>
> —— Richard J. Evans, *In Defence of History*

Achievement in Context

In Defence of History was directly shaped by the intellectual climate in British universities in the late twentieth century. It was written in the wake of what Evans saw as the disarray and "impotence" of the academic left, "underlined by the crisis of academia which began in the 1970s and reached its height in the 1980s."[4] Evans provided a way of understanding postmodernism as a product of these transitions, and reassured fellow scholars that it would soon settle into more of a subfield or subspecialism of history "rather than revolutioniz[ing] its theory and practice as a whole."[5] Although it is linked to a specific time and place, the broad scope of the book and its central theme—related to a universal question about historical validity—remains useful for students, teachers, and the wider public.

A cornerstone of Evans's position is his assertion that the treatment of historical material has important implications beyond academia. Notably, Evans served as an expert witness in the historian Deborah Lipstadt's* libel defense against the Holocaust*–denier David Irving* in 2000. Lipstadt was described in *In Defence of History* as the "leading authority" on Holocaust denial, and Evans echoed her concerns that conspiracy theories and "revisionism" (challenges to historical orthodoxy) had flourished in the United States in the 1990s when "attacks on the Western rationalist tradition have become fashionable."[6] During the trial he was asked to comment on the historical accuracy of Irving's work. Evans condemned Irving, showing how Irving's account of the Holocaust failed the test of honest and faithful scholarship, legitimizing Lipstadt's accusations. For Evans, it was futile to make excuses for Holocaust denial by invoking postmodern theories. "Auschwitz* was not a discourse," Evans insists. "It trivializes mass murder to see it as a text."[7]

Limitations

Although *In Defence of History* could have been useful in other subjects where postmodern ideas have provided a challenge to existing ideas and conventions—such as literary studies, art, economics, linguistics, architecture, and philosophy—Evans does not engage at length with the philosophy of postmodern thinkers. For many, this failure to analyze the views of his opponents fully is a major weakness of the text. The English literary critic Stefan Collini,* writing in the *Guardian*, complained that the book was superficial in its analysis, featuring "vulgarized rebuttals of vulgarized ideas."[8] Yet Evans turned this criticism into a compliment: "If by vulgarized, he means 'popularized', then I gladly plead guilty."[9] He was not writing for those who were experts in the realm of theory, but those who were engaging with these concepts on a practical level as an extension to their research, and lay readers without access to the specialized and sometimes opaque language used by postmodern thinkers. His hatred of postmodern jargon explains Evans's desire to translate these complex debates into more accessible language and challenge them in more transparent terms. Yet Collini's insight that Evans's desire to be popular came at the expense of any serious engagement with postmodern philosophy can still be considered valid.

Unsurprisingly, academics within those disciplines such as literary studies, which were more compatible with deconstruction* (an approach to cultural analysis that states, very roughly, that meaning is dependent on language) and postmodernism, complained that Evans had not engaged sufficiently with the theorists he was criticizing. Catherine Belsey,* a respected interpreter of contemporary philosophy, accused Evans of extolling the virtues of close reading, yet in practice misquoting and misunderstanding complex writers like the philosopher Jacques Derrida* and the literary theorist Roland Barthes.* For Belsey, Evans sacrificed real engagement with these thinkers, preferring to present his antagonists as a series of "bogeys" or "intellectual monsters to frighten the credulous."[10]

---

1. "Richard J Evans—*In Defence of History*," *Kirkus Reviews*, November 1, 1998, accessed July 23, 2015, https://www.kirkusreviews.com/book-reviews/richard-j-evans/in-defence-of-history/.
2. Richard J. Evans, *In Defence of History*, 2nd ed. (London, Granta, 2001), 316.
3. Evans, *In Defence of History*, 254.
4. Evans, *In Defence of History*, 198.
5. Evans, *In Defence of History*, 203.
6. Evans, *In Defence of History*, 241.
7. Evans, *In Defence of History*, 124.
8. Stefan Collini, "The Truth Vandals," *Guardian*, December 18, 1997, 15.
9. Evans, *In Defence of History*, 256.
10. Catherine Belsey, "In Defence of History," *European Journal of English Studies* 3, no. 1 (1999): 108.

MODULE 8
PLACE IN THE AUTHOR'S WORK

KEY POINTS

• Evans's historical practice largely deals with modern Germany, although he has gone on to provide broader interventions on historical method.

• *In Defence of History* draws heavily on his background with the social history* of Germany, and informs his later profile as a public historian.

• More recently, Evans expands his position against nationalist histories in *Cosmopolitan Islanders* (2005), a study of the traditions of European historical practice in twentieth-century Britain.

Positioning

In Defence of History was published in September 1997, when Richard J. Evans was 50 years old and had already produced a number of historical works, primarily concerned with modern German history. As a student in Oxford he had taken a particular interest in the controversy surrounding the work of Fritz Fischer,* a historian who placed responsibility on the Germans for the outbreak of World War I.*¹ Evans developed a passion for social history, providing a significant contribution to this area with his first book *The Feminist Movement in Germany 1894–1933* (1976).² His major work *Death in Hamburg* (1987) dealt with the social and political implications of cholera outbreaks in the city between 1830 and 1910,³ while *Rituals of Retribution* (1997) considered the use of capital punishment in Germany between 1600 and 1987.⁴

This background in German social history was fundamental to

In Defence of History, and allowed Evans to illustrate his opposition to the implications of postmodernism* in relation to the study of the Holocaust.* While postmodernists maintain that conventional history is always the story of "the winner," often neglecting the narratives of marginalized groups, Evans regards this generalization as a myth, noting that "it is precisely the poor and the unknown, the losers and indeed, the female, who have attracted the largest number of historians and been the subject of the greatest number of books."[5] Since *In Defence in History* was published in 1997, Evans has increasingly moved away from the study of late nineteenth-century Germany to produce an important trilogy on Nazi Germany.*[6] But he has continued to make interventions on historiographical* issues that have reached not just other historians of Germany but all members of the discipline. As part of his appointment as Regius Professor of History at Cambridge, Evans delivered his inaugural lectures in 2009 on the theme of British historians of the European continent—a tradition to which he has made a notable impact.[7]

> "Total relativism provides no objective criteria by which fascist and racist views of history can be falsified ... The increase in scope and intensity of the Holocaust deniers' activities since the mid-1970s has among other things reflected the postmodern intellectual climate, above all in the USA, in which scholars have increasingly denied that texts had any fixed meaning, and have argued instead that the meaning is supplied by the reader, and in which attacks on the Western rationalist tradition have become fashionable."
> —— Richard J. Evans, *In Defence of History*

Integration

During the 1970s, Evans was one of a number of young British social historians who posed a challenge to the established view of Wilhelmine Germany* (1871–1918).[8] British social historians like Evans helped effect a shift in focus away from the consideration of high politics, the state, and Prussian dominance over other German states to include more complex social relations.[9] The group was influenced by the "New Left,"* an intellectual movement concerned with examining "history from below"[10] (that is, conducting research on individuals and communities previously considered to be inconsequential). Part of Evans's approach to history was to highlight "the importance of the grassroots of politics and the everyday life and experience of ordinary people."[11] Undermining the view that postmodernism provided a novel intervention on behalf of the oppressed, Evans makes it clear within *In Defence of History* that social history as it was already being practiced took up the mission to expose "fundamental structures of inequality in society."[12]

German history also exemplified for Evans why doing history fairly was a matter of civic responsibility. He had participated in the *Historikerstreit** (the "historians' quarrel" provoked by conservative historians who wanted to challenge the "guilt" felt by many German people) and hence observed how politically sensitive scholarly questions related to objectivity* and empathy could be. *In Hitler's Shadow* (1989) saw Evans tackling the awkwardness many German historians felt in coming to terms with the legacies of the Nazi regime, once again highlighting their potential as scholars to shape public debate.[13] This view informed *In Defence of History*, since Evans feared that postmodernism threatened to undermine historians' social obligations to seek and represent the truth; he applied this in his role as an expert witness in the libel trial lost by the Holocaust–denier and author David Irving* in 2000. The following year he reflected on the case to draw wider lessons about historians in the public sphere for his book *Telling Lies about Hitler*.[14]

Significance

The continuing influence of *In Defence of History* can still be noted in many university reading lists, and the book is currently in its 12th printing. It has also been translated into 12 languages—clear evidence of its relevance outside the United Kingdom. Despite the large volume of criticism the work received from both traditionalist and postmodern historians, Evans has done little to modify his position. In fact, he addresses his critics directly in a scathing Afterword appended to the book's 2000 edition. While the work remains less respected by scholars than his earlier research on social history—such as the classic *Death in Hamburg*—it is undoubtedly the book by Evans that has been most widely read and most hotly debated. His introduction to the fortieth anniversary edition of E. H. Carr's *What Is History?* in 2001 celebrates the work's continuing resonance.[15]

 The postmodern challenge that seemed so threatening in the 1990s largely receded in the following decade. But some of the positions Evans opposes in *In Defence of History* have recurred. Evans was bitterly critical of intellectual nationalism, attacking G. R. Elton's* assumption that historians should concentrate on writing the history of the nation-state they happen to live in. Evans lamented that historians in Germany and France had generally proven to be "obstinately insular"—that is, inward-looking—when it came to studying other cultures. By contrast, Evans hailed the contribution of British and American scholars who had written momentous historical works on other countries.[16]

This theme was revived in his 2009 book Cosmopolitan Islanders. Here Evans praises the success of those English-speaking scholars who combine deep research with readability and skill in writing, and warns against the potential of a new intellectual isolationism resulting from the decline of teaching foreign languages in schools.[17]

---

1. Daniel Snowman, "Daniel Snowman Meets the Historian of Germany, Defender of History and Expert Witness in the Irving Trial," *History Today* 54 (2004): 45.
2. Richard J. Evans, *The Feminist Movement in Germany 1894–1933* (London: Sage Publications, 1976).
3. Richard J. Evans, *Death in Hamburg: Society and Politics in the Cholera Years, 1830–1910* (Oxford: Clarendon Press, 1987).
4. Richard J. Evans, *Rituals of Retribution: Capital Punishment in Germany 1600–1987* (Oxford: Oxford University Press, 1996).
5. Richard J. Evans, *In Defence of History*, 2nd ed. (London, Granta, 2001), 212.
6. Richard J. Evans, *The Coming of the Third Reich* (London: Allen Lane, 2003); *The Third Reich in Power, 1933–1939* (London: Allen Lane, 2005); *The Third Reich at War 1939–1945* (London: Allen Lane, 2008).

7. Richard J. Evans, *Cosmopolitan Islanders: British Historians and the European Continent* (Cambridge: Cambridge University Press, 2009).
8. Theodor S. Hamerow, "Guilt, Redemption and Writing German History," *The American Historical Review* 88, February (1983): 65–70.
9. Richard J. Evans, "Introduction: Wilhelm II's Germany and the Historians," in Richard J. Evans, *Society and Politics in Wilhelmine Germany* (London: Croom Helm, 1978), 11–39.
10. Hamerow, "Guilt, Redemption and Writing German History," 70.
11. Evans, "Introduction: Wilhelm II's Germany and the Historians," 22–3.
12. Evans, *In Defence of History*, 212.
13. Richard J. Evans, *In Hitler's Shadow: West German Historians and the Attempt to Escape from the Nazi Past* (London: I.B. Tauris, 1989).
14. Richard J. Evans, *Telling Lies about Hitler: The Holocaust, History and the David Irving Trial* (London: Verso, 2001).
15. See E.H. Carr, *What Is History?* Introduced by Richard J. Evans (Basingstoke: Palgrave, 40th anniversary ed., 2001).
16. Evans, *In Defence of History*, 179–81.
17. See A.W. Purdue, "Book of the Week: *Cosmopolitan Islanders*," *Times Higher Education*, July 9, 2009, accessed October 24, 2013, http://www.timeshighereducation.co.uk/407279.article.

SECTION 3
IMPACT

MODULE 9
THE FIRST RESPONSES

KEY POINTS

* The most potent critique of Evans's position regards his view of objectivity* and the pursuit of truth—concepts the postmodernists* wished to expose as outdated.
* Critics of *In Defence* came from both traditional empiricists* and postmodernists; Evans replied by accusing his critics of being politically motivated, and showed how they in turn had misunderstood his arguments.
* This was a significant quarrel between academics, with clashes of personality sometimes taking greater prominence than the philosophical debate.

Criticism

Richard J. Evans's *In Defence of History* was intended to navigate a middle course between a traditional empiricist approach to history and the challenge of postmodern theories to the validity of the discipline—approaches with different understandings of the possibility of discovering objective truth through historical research. His work came under a great deal of scrutiny from both camps, though it had an essentially favorable reception.

Among Evans's more politically motivated critics was the conservative historian Niall Ferguson.* In Ferguson's view, history did not need defending, as it was more popular in British educational institutions than ever. Ferguson insists that the work is "rude" to historians of a "broadly conservative nature."[1] Evans's central concerns and approach to social history,* which grew out of his position within the "New Left"* in his early academic career, seem fundamentally incompatible with the Ferguson's broadly right-wing stance.²

Postmodernists criticized Evans's refusal to engage with postmodern philosophy in its own terms, misunderstanding and misrepresenting their field of thought as well as individual thinkers. Furthermore, many insisted that *In Defence of History* promoted an outdated concept of objectivity, defending conservative approaches to history, and advancing contradictory arguments. Particularly fierce criticism was leveled by the historian Keith Jenkins,* who is a key target of Evans's intellectual attacks. In *Why History?*, Jenkins devotes a chapter to Evans's work, noting that his defense of history is part of a conservative, bourgeois structure, and that his work is intended to defend not history itself, but Evans's own position in academia within a "History Club."³

Further critiques provoked by Evans's work were quite diverse. For instance, the American historian Joyce Appleby* suggests that Evans's argument is entirely unnecessary, seeing the postmodern rejection of the pursuit of objective truth in historical practice as too untenable to warrant so much attention.⁴ Lynn Hunt,* an American scholar noted for her work in the theory of history, criticizes Evans for his constant references to outmoded debates between scholars such as G. R. Elton* and E. H. Carr.*⁵ The scholar Anthony Easthope,* noted for his interest in contemporary literary theory, uses Evans's final paragraph, based on Carr's final paragraph in *What Is History?*, as evidence of a fundamental agreement with empiricist objectivity.

> "I have been taken aback by the sheer variety and by the utterly contradictory nature of the responses which the book has elicited. I would not have thought it possible for a single book to be read, or misread, in so many different ways."
> —— Richard J. Evans, Afterword to *In Defence of History*

Responses

Evans responded to his critics in detail through the website of the Institute of Historical Research, London, between 1998 and 1999; these responses formed the basis for an Afterword which has appeared in editions of the work since 2000.

Evans convincingly defends against most critiques of his work. While he acknowledges Easthope's point about a few factual errors, he refutes other critics and accuses many of misreading his work. According to Evans, Jenkins ascribes views to Evans that he doesn't hold (and mistakenly characterizes all historians as a homogeneous elite), depicting Evans's stance on objectivity as traditionally empiricist.[6] While Evans notes the importance of some of the nineteenth-century German historian Leopold von Ranke's* method in research, throughout the book he asserts his belief in a limited objectivity in which the subjectivity of the historian plays an integral part.[7]

Diane Purkiss,* a postmodern historian notable for her work in gender and witchcraft, had accused Evans of holding conservative views and misrepresenting her work.[8] Defending his treatment of individual historians like Ferguson and Purkiss, Evans noted that he only used the words of the authors themselves, representing them fairly in his book. He argued that throughout the book he is clearly in favor of diversity and plurality in history, including some postmodern ideas. The work is intended to defend the links between the practice of writing history and the accurate representation of the past, not any particular school.

Conflict and Consensus

Evans admitted that he had made the odd "howler" in his treatment of a philosopher or theorist.[9] Yet in general he held his ground, and stubbornly pointed out the almost "comical" way that his book had been misread or misunderstood.[10] Evans insisted that his postmodern enemies had become "so angry" precisely because he had exposed their sham political posturing, and carefully detailed each of the ways in which they had misrepresented or willfully twisted his arguments.[11] Some of the phrases that infuriated them, such as the description of postmodernists as "intellectual barbarians," were left in the manuscript by Evans because "I didn't believe anyone would be stupid enough" to take the expression literally.[12] Such bad-tempered and derisory exchanges meant that there was little reconciliation between Evans and his critics.

The debate often touched on personal invective and academic rivalry, rather than clarifying important philosophical points. Doug Munro,* a scholar noted for his work in historical biography, comments, in a generally positive review, that while Evans plausibly defends himself from accusations of adherence to Elton's views on national history or gender history, these have nothing to do with his view on objectivity, which is sometimes unclear.[13]

Similarly, Evans's position on causality is weak, and his adherence to many of Carr's ideas is an area that can be questioned. As Jenkins noted, Evans did not answer how causation works in practice and how one can successfully select a hierarchy of causes.[14]

The wide criticism from different quarters suggests that a consensus has not been reached on this popular work. This is perhaps to be expected; *In Defence of History* aims to refute a number of important and contradictory schools of thought and offers Evans's critical analysis of the work of individuals.

---

1. Niall Ferguson, "History Is Dead, Long Live History!," *Sunday Times*, September 21, 1997.
2. Richard J. Evans, *In Defence of History*, 2nd ed. (London: Granta, 2001), 261.
3. Keith Jenkins, *Why History? Ethics and Postmodernity* (London: Routledge, 1999), 106–12.
4. Joyce Appleby, "Does It Really Need Defending?," *The Times Literary Supplement*, October 31, 1997: 10.
5. Lynn Hunt, "Does History Need Defending?," *History Workshop Journal* 46, December (1998): 241–9.
6. Evans, *In Defence of History*, 277–85.
7. Evans, *In Defence of History*, 271–2.
8. Diane Purkiss, "A Response to Richard J. Evans," *History in Focus*, accessed October 24, 2013, http://www.history.ac.uk/ihr/Focus/Whatishistory/purkiss1.html. See also Diane Purkiss, *The Witch in History: Early Modern and Twentieth-Century Representations* (London: Routledge, 1996).
9. Evans, *In Defence of History*, 292.
10. Evans, "Afterword" to *In Defence of History*, 270.
11. Evans, "Afterword" to *In Defence of History*, 285.
12. Evans, *In Defence of History*, 296.
13. Doug Munro, "*In Defence of History* (Review)," *Journal of Social History* 36, no. 1 (2002): 242–4.
14. Jenkins, "On Richard Evans" in *Why History?*, 105.

MODULE 10
THE EVOLVING DEBATE

KEY POINTS

- Evans's work is regarded by some as an important but now superseded contribution, and some worry that his arguments endorse hostility to contemporary theoretical approaches to cultural analysis.
- Evans's writing on the history of historians belongs to a wider trend of studying the growth of the discipline, and considering its social role.
- The text has had a huge impact on undergraduate courses; elements of postmodern* theory such as attention to style and self-reflexivity (an awareness of the role of the researcher in the process of analysis) on the part of authors have largely been assimilated into the profession.

Uses and Problems

Richard J. Evans's *In Defence of History* can be seen as a work that not only engaged in the debate about history, but also spread the debate to a new audience inside—and beyond—professional academia. Since its publication, Evans's book has been noted in other works, such as the British historians John Tosh's* *Why History Matters* (2008) and Ludmilla Jordanova's* *History in Practice* (2006).[1] These books provide a useful introduction for students into historiographical* debates, although their approach is less polemical and argumentative, as the challenge from postmodernism seems less urgent, beyond the particular flashpoints such as Holocaust* denial.

Tosh and Jordanova are open to theoretical approaches, and want to distance themselves from the perceived conservatism of Evans's case for objectivity.* Tosh dismissively remarked in his 1999 review that Evans is speaking from "somewhere near the dead center of the profession," espousing an argument that would be endorsed by "the overwhelming majority" of fellow historians. Tosh is clearly disappointed by the work's "surprising conservative" conclusions in light of Evans's previous reputation at "the cutting edge of social history."[2] Indeed, for those historians who believe in the benefits of engaging with theory, there were anxieties that Evans's defense of empiricism* might actually turn students away from more conceptual thinking. As the historian R. D. Anderson* observed in 2001: "On the whole, British students do not need to be warned against the excesses of theory; the problem is rather to arouse an interest in more than the most empirical approach, and it would be a pity if Evans's book was thought to legitimize anti-theoretical attitudes."[3] While many historians would agree with Evans about the dangers of extreme relativism,* and the associated idea that objectivity is impossible to achieve, they were wary in case *In Defence of History* was used as a way of trying to close off conversation with other disciplines.

> "Like other new approaches to history, therefore, postmodern theory would seem to be more applicable to some areas of history than others. A recognition of this likelihood is the first step in the direction of harnessing its more positive ideas to the research and writing of history in the twenty-first century."
> —— Richard J. Evans, *In Defence of History*

Schools of Thought

While *In Defence of History* is important, particularly for students, teachers, and some historians, its influence on the intellectual practice of history has declined in the last few years. Many of the ideas within the work can be traced to other historians and were already well established in the mainstream of historical thought. What this book offered instead was a new and outspoken defense of existing practices of history, and it raised important questions about the public role and visibility of historians. This has become a vital topic in light of the popularity of historical programming on British television and the commercial appeal of history publishing, as well as historians' roles in advising on curriculum reform. *In Defence of History* has been followed by a number of books reflecting on how historians communicate their research with a broad audience, and how their scholarship impacts upon broader representations of the past.[4]

The overview given by Evans of the development of the historical profession belongs to a wider fascination with the history of history over the past three decades.[5] Sometimes this had led to attempts to revive the importance of particular historians. For instance, the historian David Cannadine* wrote a very admiring tribute to the popular early twentieth-century British historian G. M. Trevelyan* (although Evans suspected that this nostalgic "patrician" writer would "continue to be neglected in the future").[6] More recently Michael Bentley* has demonstrated "modernist" approaches that revitalized historiography* in Britain in the early twentieth century—drawing attention to shared patterns of thought and stylistic techniques.[7] But it has also led to a greater awareness of the different media through which historical narratives are communicated in the modern world—including theatre, film, TV, and radio—and how these narratives inform cultural memory.[8] As one of the most prominent and decorated historians in Britain, Evans illustrates and commentates on the growing presence of historians in public life.

In Current Scholarship

While many of the ideas expressed in the work are not new or at the cutting edge, *In Defence of History* has had a significant impact on the field of history and has been cited in many subsequent works. The book outlines a general defense for history as a discipline against extreme postmodern challenges, rather than for any specific methodology or subject of study. As such, the scope of the work is perhaps too wide-ranging to have inspired the formation of any specific schools. Nonetheless it has been cited in numerous recent discussions of historical method: these include a 2012 article on the use of archives, a 2010 article examining various defenses of historical inquiry, and a 2000 article on history, the Holocaust, and historiography.[9]

The force of Evans's argument against certain aspects of postmodern theory may cause some readers to assume he rejects all postmodern ideas. Keith Jenkins* suggests that while Evans appears to be conciliatory toward some elements of postmodern thinking, this is merely a tactic used to mask his antipathy towards its ideas.[10] Yet Evans, by contrast, insisted on the benefits that could be gained by adopting some of postmodernism's methodological questions, while rejecting its corrosive ideas about the impossibility of reaching truth.[11] To that extent, Evans predicted that postmodernism could be tempered and assimilated as a "legitimate sub specialism." He compared the process to that by which rock and roll started as a form of youth revolt but was co-opted into simply being a musical style, shorn of its radical edge.[12] And in this Evans has been vindicated. Postmodern scholarship has been incorporated into some university departments, just as postmodern ideas have been integrated into the arsenal of historian's approaches.

---

1. John Tosh, *Why History Matters* (Basingstoke: Palgrave Macmillan, 2008); Ludmilla Jordanova, *History in Practice*, 2nd edn (London: Hodder Arnold, 2006).
2. John Tosh, "Shorter Note: In Defence of History," *The English Historical Review* 114 (1999): 805.
3. R. D. Anderson, "Reviews: In Defence of History," *The Scottish Historical Review* 79 (2000): 106.
4. Peter Mandler, *History and National Life* (London: Profile Books, 2002).
5. John Burrow, *A History of Histories: Epics, Chronicles, Romances and Inquiries from Herodotus to the Twentieth Century* (London: Penguin, 2009).
6. David Cannadine, *G.M. Trevelyan: A Life in History* (London: Fontana, 1993); Richard J. Evans, *In Defence of History*, 2nd ed. (London, Granta, 2001), 163.
7. Michael Bentley, *Modernizing England's Pasts: English Historiography in the Age of Modernism 1870–1970* (Cambridge: Cambridge University Press, 2006).
8. Raphael Samuel, *Theatres of Memory: Past and Present in Contemporary Culture*, vol. 1 (London: Verso, 1996).
9. Mary Lindeman, "The Discreet Charm of the Diplomatic Archive," *German History: The Journal of the German History Society*, 29, no. 2 (2011): 283–304; Alexander Lyon Macfie, "On the Defence of (My) History," *Rethinking History: The Journal of Theory and Practice* 14, no. 2 (2010): 209–27;

and Michael Dintenfass, "Truth's Other: Ethics, the History of the Holocaust, and Historiographical Theory after the Linguistic Turn," *History and Theory* 39, no. 1 (2000): 1–20.
10. Keith Jenkins, *Why History? Ethics and Postmodernity* (London: Routledge, 1999), 95–114.
11. Evans, *In Defence of History*, 156.
12. Evans, *In Defence of History*, 203.

MODULE 11
IMPACT AND INFLUENCE TODAY

KEY POINTS
- Although *In Defence of History* is still important for undergraduates as an introduction to the methods available to historians, it is not seen as a source of groundbreaking ideas.
- The text contributed to a broader backlash against postmodernism* and the cultural turn* in the early 2000s.
- Evans has been criticized for resorting to polemical attacks—aggressive criticism—and has failed to fully engage with postmodern philosophers.

Position

Richard J. Evans's *In Defence of History* is still used to highlight the controversy concerning the nature of history for university students. This was a central aim of the book and, in this regard, the criticism of the work has enhanced its usefulness. It has further widened the general debate relating to history and brought more students into contact with the key questions of objectivity,* causation, and how history is practiced. Yet these philosophical questions have been bound up in a very polemical exchange of accusations. One reviewer reflected that in the Afterword, in which Evans gives a lengthy rebuttal to his critics, he came across as "petulant and thin-skinned," displaying a "touchy defensiveness" and often resorting to "distasteful" personal attacks.[1]

While the text received great attention at the time of publication and remains a valuable work on the nature of history, less attention has been paid to it in more recent times. Perhaps unsurprisingly, postmodernists like Keith Jenkins* and Alun Munslow* decided to exclude Evans from their 2004 anthology compiled of 45 different historians, *The Nature of History Reader*.[2] More conventional historians have found the work too broad, and too lacking in originality, to make a decisive contribution. As John Tosh* notes in his 2008 work *Why History Matters*, Evans does not provide any social justification for history or suggest how it could be linked to the wider public.[3] *In Defence of History* is concerned with defending existing ideas of history rather than fully outlining a new practice of history. Yet Evans clearly believes that historians can play a public role in correcting lies told about the Holocaust,* as seen in his role in the libel trial lost by the Holocaust–denier David Irving.*

> "Stimulating debate was one of the book's principal aims; it was never intended to close down discussion (nor would that have been feasible in any case). As those who have attacked the book for failing to confront the major postmodernist thinkers have rightly if somewhat superfluously pointed out, the issues at stake cannot be settled in a couple of hundred pages. So it is important that the debate continues."
> —— Richard J. Evans, Afterword to *In Defence of History*

Interaction

The work continues to ask its readers, both inside and outside academia, to consider the impact of theories that suggest that the reality of the past is secondary or unimportant. For instance, Evans challenges the claim of the Australian scholar Diane Purkiss* that historians should relate the experiences of Jews in Auschwitz* because these stories are so morally "moving"—yet, he writes, "does it really not matter whether or not they are true?"[4] Evans maintains that the scholarly rigor and historical method play an important part in accurately remembering the past and the suffering experienced by individuals.

The "cultural turn" seemed all-powerful in the early 1990s, and introduced many important concepts from French continental philosophy into mainstream historical writing. Yet in the 2000s there have been signs of a backlash against the excesses of histories based purely on discourse—"texts" formed by systems of assumptions and statements—and representation, even among its former champions such as Lynn Hunt.*[5]

Historians in a range of fields sought to find some way of connecting language and discourse back to the lived, social environment (what Evans called "a restoration of a real historical context to language and to thought").[6] This did not necessarily mean turning away from theory. Rather, as distinguished cultural historians like Peter Mandler* suggested, it meant drawing on a wider range of theories and using them in a more critical and pragmatic way. Part of the "problem with cultural history," as Mandler saw it, was that historians had overlooked the "throw" of cultural forms. In other words, they had become too invested in describing discourses and not spent enough time working out why certain discourses were believed, and by which groups, while others were not.[7]

The Continuing Debate

The response from advocates of postmodern philosophy to Evans's work displayed a mixture of intellectual, personal, and political elements. While the point of contention was the intellectual dispute about the concept of objectivity, other criticisms appeared based on individuals' personal resentment toward their treatment in *In Defence of History*. This was due in part to Evans's polemical style. Diane Purkiss described Evans's description of her as a postmodernist* as "hysterical" and accused him of belonging to a "conservative argufying machine."[8] Although Evans's robust Afterword allows him to deal at length with rival historians, it is clear that he failed to deal sufficiently with the intellectual contribution of thinkers such as Roland Barthes* and Jacques Derrida,* especially noted for their theories relating to language and meaning. The historian R. D. Anderson* regrets that Evans leaves so many "gaps in the picture," especially missing the opportunity to engage constructively with the work of the French social theorist and historian Michel Foucault,* who should have been closest to Evans as a "historian of disease and crime."[9]

Another serious omission from Evans's account is anti-colonial and postcolonial theory. And yet some of the most trenchant attacks on the authority of the historical discipline have come from those scholars who want first to recover the experience of subordinate groups, and second to reframe the way that history is narrated to give equal voice to the colonizers and the colonized. The work of Derrida has been highly influential in this sphere too, with literary critics and historians influenced by deconstruction* describing the existing practice of history as a "white mythology."[10] For some postcolonial thinkers (that is, thinkers dealing with the various social, historical, and literary legacies of colonialism), this means a concerted effort to "provincialize Europe," in order to find ways of writing history that do not reproduce oppressive Western hierarchies.[11] While *In Defence of History* was effective in fighting off the challenge to notions of objectivity that came from postmodernist relativism*—the idea, roughly, that it is impossible to arrive any objective "truth" through historical research—it does not deal with the methodological challenges that are emerging out of new postcolonial approaches to, and criticisms of, historical research.

1. Doug Munro, "*In Defence of History* (review)," *Journal of Social History* 36, no. 1 (2002): 242.
2. Keith Jenkins and Alun Munslow, *The Nature of History Reader* (London: Routledge, 2004).
3. John Tosh, *Why History Matters* (Basingstoke: Palgrave Macmillan, 2008), 18.
4. Richard J. Evans, *In Defence of History*, 2nd ed. (London, Granta, 2001), 242.
5. Lynn Hunt, Victoria Bonnell, and Richard Biernacki, eds., *Beyond the Cultural Turn: New Directions in the Study of Society and Culture* (Berkeley, CA: University of California Press, 1999).
6. Evans, *In Defence of History*, 217.
7. Peter Mandler, "The Problem with Cultural History, or is Playtime Over?," *Cultural and Social History* 1, no. 1 (2004): 94–117.
8. Diane Purkiss, "A Response to Richard J. Evans," *History in Focus*, accessed October 24, 2013, http://www.history.ac.uk/ihr/Focus/ Whatishistory/purkiss1.html. See also Evans, *In Defence of History*, 304, 307.
9. R. D. Anderson, "Review: In Defence of History," *The Scottish Historical Review* 79 (2000): 106.
10. Robert Young, *White Mythologies: Writing, History and the West* (London: Routledge, 1990).
11. Dipesh Chakrabarty, *Provincializing Europe: Postcolonial Thought and Historical Difference* (Princeton, N.J.: Princeton University Press, 2000).

MODULE 12
WHERE NEXT?

KEY POINTS

* *In Defence of History* continues to matter for undergraduate teaching, and retains its importance among the general public as an example of why historians should uphold truthful versions of the past.
* Although it does not present a new mode of studying and writing history, the text has illustrated the diversity in historical practice and theory.
* The impact of *In Defence of History* has been diminishing with the growth of world and global history.

Potential

Since the publication of Richard J. Evans's *In Defence of History* in 1997, the fear that postmodernism* might provide a new paradigm (an overarching intellectual framework inside which solutions to research problems are solved) for historical research has entirely receded—although aspects of postmodern thinking can still be found in American journals like *Representations* and *History & Theory*, where the Dutch philosopher of history Frank Ankersmit* is on the editorial board. There has been a backlash even in literary and philosophical circles against the obsession with describing all social phenomena as an approximation of a literary text. As Evans noted, this analogy does not work, as "most of the time, the majority of people are neither readers nor writers."[1] Beyond this, the 2000s have seen a deeper appreciation of materiality across the humanities—that is, thinkers have been looking at those physical, tactile, embodied forms of knowledge that cannot be reduced to mere discourse.²

In Defence of History also made clear the public responsibilities of the historian to uphold truth against distortion—a subject with particular relevance and sensitivity in Germany. This theme is addressed by Evans's new book, *The Third Reich in History and Memory* (2015), a collection of his journalism and book reviews, mapping how interpretations of Nazism* have evolved over the past 20 years. Evans shows how the increasing "global turn"* in scholarship—a turn toward the writing of global histories, connecting geographically divided research areas—has led Nazism to be compared to other forms of European empire-building, and, more controversially, how the Holocaust* has been compared to other forms of genocide. Evans weighs the benefits and the dangers of such interpretations, and the collection as a whole testifies to Evans's belief that historians have an ethical duty to describe the past as honestly and responsibly as possible.³

> "Historians not only deconstruct the narratives of other historians, they also deconstruct the narratives of the past as well."
> —— Richard J. Evans, *In Defence of History*

Future Directions

In Defence of History describes how the geographical horizon of historians has dramatically expanded since the 1960s. Against skeptics such as G. R. Elton* and Hugh Trevor–Roper,* some historians moved away from prioritizing the history of their own nation or the history of the West to look instead at broader international connections. "Historical scholarship is thus not only more eclectic than ever before," Evans observed approvingly, "it is also becoming gradually less Eurocentric* in its coverage and approach."[4] Yet this very broadening has brought with it fresh problems. For one thing, the growing interest in imperial history has done nothing to reverse the decline in the study of foreign languages in British schools. When Evans published *Cosmopolitan Islanders* in 2009, he wanted to vindicate a tradition of scholarship about Europe that now seemed to be under threat.[5] Second, the big questions about historical method have shifted away from objectivity* and relativism* (central to the postmodernist challenge) to consider how to integrate and do justice to the diverse and often violent experiences of different parts of the globe.[6]

This global dimension has encouraged the pursuit of "big history"—a trend toward considering much longer time-spans and much bigger geographical units than in conventional historical narratives. Evans's own admiration for the influential *Annales* school,* noted for its approach to social history, and disdain for lazy periodization might make him sympathetic to such an approach.[7] The most passionate advocate of this "big history" approach, the Harvard historian David Armitage,* co-authored *The History Manifesto* (2014), aiming to set a new agenda for the discipline. His recommendations include tackling deliberately big data and deliberately big questions, in order to prove the relevance and usefulness of history for government policy.[8] The manifesto has been hugely divisive and subject to extensive and vitriolic criticism.[9] This is a reminder, perhaps, of the difficulties any single scholar faces in trying to define and speak for a historical profession that has become so diverse in its outlook.

Summary

In Defence of History deserves special attention as a passionate, lucid, and entertaining attempt to defend history from postmodern challenges. In the 1980s and 1990s new philosophies of language were applied to the study of history by scholars such as Hayden White,* Frank Ankersmit,* and Keith Jenkins.* Within the work, Evans outlines why history remains a valid discipline. While he recognizes the inescapable role of present-day preoccupations and the force of the historical imagination, Evans insists that the documents that historians use can give them a direct connection to events and people in the past. Evans proposes that some limited form of objectivity is indeed possible, since the nature of the evidence places constrictions on what the historian can say. While good historians will possess "poetry and imagination" in the way they question their sources, documentary evidence allows this to be "disciplined by fact."[10]

While the text is heavily influenced by earlier works of historical theory, especially the Marxist* historian E. H. Carr's* *What Is History?*, its consideration of the "linguistic turn"* and postmodern challenge brings these older arguments up to date for a new generation. However, it is a defense of the mainstream practice of history and, as such, is not a revolutionary work. The text is important because it addresses postmodernism—which questions the purpose, validity, and practices of history—and provides students and teachers with an effective entry point to the debate surrounding the discipline. One of Evans's motivations for writing the book was to indicate that postmodernism can lead to an extreme form of relativism that tolerates fascist and racist ideas, even Holocaust denial. This warning grew directly out of Evans's status as a preeminent social historian* of Germany. The work retains its importance for generating a wide-ranging, sometimes acrimonious, conversation between historians about the purposes and conventions of their profession.

---

1. Richard J. Evans, *In Defence of History*, 2nd ed. (London, Granta: 2001), 186.
2. For an introduction, see Daniel Miller, *Materiality* (Durham, NC: Duke University Press, 2005).
3. Richard J. Evans, *The Third Reich in History and Memory* (New York: Little, Brown, 2015).
4. Evans, *In Defence of History*, 181.
5. Richard J. Evans, *Cosmopolitan Islanders: British Historians and the European Continent* (Cambridge: Cambridge University Press, 2009).
6. Dipesh Chakrabharti, *Provincializing Europe: Postcolonial Thought and Historical Difference* (Princeton: Princeton University Press, 2000).
7. Evans, *In Defence of History*, 156.
8. David Armitage and Jo Guldi, *The History Manifesto* (Cambridge: Cambridge University Press, 2014). Available online: http://historymanifesto.cambridge.org/.
9. Peter Mandler, Deborah Cohen, "The History Manifesto: A Critique," *American Historical Review* 120, no. 2 (2015): 530–42.
10. Evans, *In Defence of History*, 251.

GLOSSARY OF TERMS

1. **Annales school:** a school of thought named after the French academic journal *Annales d'Histoire Économique et Sociale*. Annales historians sought the creation of history that drew on the aims and methods of different academic disciplines and encompassed the social, psychological, and economic past. Important writers within the Annales include Marc Bloch, Lucien Febvre, and Ferdinand Braudel.

2. **Anti-Semitism:** hostility or prejudice towards Jewish people.

3. **Auschwitz:** a concentration and extermination camp in Nazi-occupied Poland that was a key site for the mass murder of millions of European Jews.

4. **Cold War (1947–1991):** a period of military and ideological tension between the capitalist United States and the communist Soviet Union between the end of World War II and 1991. While the two blocs never engaged in direct military conflict, they engaged in covert and proxy wars and espionage against one another.

5. **Cultural turn:** refers to the vogue for cultural historical approaches in the 1980s and early 1990s. The cultural turn was inspired in part by bringing history into closer relationship with neighboring disciplines like literary criticism, art history, and social anthropology.

6. **Deconstruction:** a movement in literary theory that began in the 1960s and questions the links between meaning and language. The French philosopher Jacques Derrida asserted that texts are inexhaustible in their possible and constantly shifting meanings.

7. **Determinism:** among historians "determinism" refers to the belief that certain developments had to occur in a particular way. Determinists discount the role of chance and instead emphasize that certain historical trends and events were necessary and inevitable.

8. **Empiricism:** a theory of knowledge that believes that the past, and its truth, can be obtained from a close examination of primary sources and evidence.

9. **Eurocentric:** a focus on European assumptions, concerns, history, and culture; historical analysis of international events that primarily considers the implications for Europe.

10. **Feminism:** a political movement that seeks to understand and overturn the enduring forms of inequality between the sexes by securing equal political, social, economic, and cultural rights for women.

11. **Global turn:** refers to the growing trends towards writing global, trans-national, and international "connective" histories in the 1990s and 2000s.

12. **Great Depression:** a global economic downturn that began in the United States following a stock-market crash in 1929.

13. *Historikerstreit:* a German term that can be translated as "the historians' quarrel." It arose in West Germany in the 1980s when several conservative historians, including Michael Stürmer and Ernst Nolte, wanted to remove the "guilt" felt by many Germans, and to revise the unique place of the Holocaust in history.

14. **Historiography:** the study of historical writing or the study of the evolution of a historical debate over time.

15. **History Workshop:** a movement founded in the 1960s by British historian Raphael Samuel. The movement favored "history from below," told from the perspective of ordinary people instead of elites.

16. **Holocaust:** the systematic, state-organized deportation and mass extermination of Jews by Nazi Germany during World War II. Some scholars argue that the mass extermination and persecution of other groups, such as socialists, homosexuals, Romani, and those with mental illnesses, should also be included in the definition.

17. **Linguistic turn:** a development in a wide number of disciplines that began to focus on the importance of language and philosophies relating to language. The "linguistic turn" was linked to poststructuralist ideas and, in particular, the work of Jacques Derrida.

18. **Marxism:** a term used to describe a broad range of approaches in a variety of different fields including history, sociology, economics, and politics. It is based upon the ideas of Karl Marx in the mid-nineteenth century. While there are various strands to Marxist thought, one of its key tenets is the belief in the

materialistic development of history, class structures, and the dialectic nature of societal forces. English Marxist historians in the mid-twentieth century include Eric Hobsbawm, Christopher Hill, and E. P. Thompson.

19. **Material turn:** a school of thought that emerged in the 1990s and 2000s. It was inspired by scholars in archaeology, art history, and anthropology. Its practitioners wanted to encourage scholars to think more about the non-discursive properties of objects and things.

20. **Meta-narrative:** a writing methodology that describe narratives that aim to give a total or comprehensive account of historical change, and suggest that history is necessarily moving in a certain progressive direction. Postmodernists have claimed that meta-narratives are oppressive or no longer relevant.

21. **Nazi Germany:** refers to the period of rule in Germany by the extremely right-wing Nationalist Socialist German Workers' (Nazi) Party led by Adolf Hitler between 1933 and 1945. Nazism is the name for the political movement and ideology created by the Nazi Party.

22. **New Left:** a term used in Britain and America to describe a movement of the late 1960s and 1970s that sought to implement wide-ranging social reforms, but rejected the approach of the traditional left-wing and Marxist parties.

23. **Objectivity:** the belief that there are real phenomena that exist, which can be judged or observed, and are independent of emotional or personal prejudices.

24. **Postmodernism:** a wide-ranging term applied to many disciplines to describe a set of beliefs that are considered to have emerged in the early twentieth century. It is usually said to include a belief that reality is a construct of the human mind. It involves an intrinsic rejection of universal laws, values, or concepts. In history, the idea of postmodernism places an emphasis on the difficulty, or impossibility, of representing the past in the present, the subjective nature of historical research, and the role of language in the historical work.

25. **Relativism:** a term given to a family of concepts that suggests there is no absolute or universal truth, knowledge, or morality, and that such ideas are intrinsically related to culture, historical circumstances, or society.

26. **Social history:** a branch of history that seeks to investigate not just the political elite but all the groups within a past society; social historians have typically been drawn to the study of different social classes, living conditions, and family relations. Influenced often by Marxism, social history saw dramatic expansion in the 1960s and 1970s, although its appeal waned in the 1980s and 1990s.

27. **Soviet Union (or USSR):** a kind of "super state" that existed from 1922 to 1991, centered primarily on Russia and its neighbors in Eastern Europe and the northern half of Asia. It was the communist pole of the Cold War, with the United States as its main "rival."

28. **Teleology:** the belief that things move inevitably towards a certain goal or end; in the case of history, teleological thinking implies that there is a purpose and a general direction driving social development.

29. **Third Reich:** the name for the regime created by Adolf Hitler and the Nazi Party in Germany between 1933 and their defeat in World War II in 1945. Intended to last a thousand years, like the first Holy Roman Empire, it lasted merely twelve.

30. **Wilhelmine Germany:** refers to Imperial Germany between 1871 and 1918, and in particular between 1888 and 1918, when it was ruled by Kasier Wilhelm II.

31. **World War I (1914–1918):** a mass conflict that began between the empires of Europe, but expanded to bring in the United States and much of the colonial world, and ended with the defeat of Germany and its allies.

32. **World War II (1939–1945):** a global conflict that ended with the Allies (Britain, France, the United States, and the Soviet Union) defeating the Axis powers (Nazi Germany, Fascist Italy, and Imperial Japan).

PEOPLE MENTIONED IN THE TEXT

1. **David Abraham** is a professor of law at the University of Miami. As a young historian in Princeton he received considerable attention for his book *The Collapse of the Weimar Republic* in 1981. The book was subject to hostile criticism for the way it manipulated sources, overlooked counter-evidence and took a partisan line to claim that big business helped bring the Nazis to power.

2. **R. D. Anderson** is a professor of history at Edinburgh University, and has worked on educational systems in France and Scotland.

3. **Joyce Appleby (b. 1929)** is an American historian who specializes in historiography and the political and economic thought of the early American Republic.

4. **Frank R. Ankersmit (b. 1945)** is a Dutch philosopher of history. He is currently professor of intellectual history and historical theory at the University of Groningen, the Netherlands.

5. **David Armitage (b. 1965)** is a historian of intellectual and international history at Harvard University. He is the joint author (with Jo Guldi) of the controversial 2014 *History Manifesto*.

6. **Roland Barthes (1915–1980)** was a French literary theorist, linguist, and philosopher. He contributed to many different theories including structuralism and post-structuralism.

7. **Catherine Belsey (b. 1940)** is a literary critic and visiting professor at the University of Derby, who has been a constant champion of innovative and postmodern theoretical approaches.

8. **Michael Bentley (b. 1948)** is a historian of Victorian British politics and twentieth-century intellectual culture.

9. **David Cannadine (b. 1950)** is a British historian who specializes in the history of nineteenth-and twentieth-century Britain, writing classic books on aristocracy, empire, and monarchy. He is also a major advisor on the teaching of history in British schools.

10. **Jane Caplan** is a historian whose main interest lies in Nazi Germany. She has

held many academic positions in both America and Britain.

11. **E. H. Carr (1892–1982)** was a British Marxist historian who wrote a classic history of interwar diplomacy and the history of the Soviet Union. His 1961 book *What Is History?* was a huge influence on Richard J. Evans.

12. **Stefan Collini (b. 1947)** is an English literary critic and professor of intellectual history at Cambridge. He specializes in British nineteenth-and twentieth-century high culture.

13. **Robert Darnton (b. 1939)** is an American historian who specializes in eighteenth-century France and the history of the book. His classic study *The Great Cat Massacre* (1984) was discussed by Richard J. Evans as an example of how some postmodern ideas could inform cultural history.

14. **Paul de Man (1919–1983)** was a Belgian-born literary theorist who settled in America and taught at Harvard. A key theorist of deconstruction, in the 1980s it was revealed that de Man had written a number of anti-Semitic articles for a collaborationist newspaper in Belgium during World War II.The resulting controversy saw Derrida and his critics trade accusations about the relationship between de Man's philosophical views and political conduct.

15. **Jacques Derrida (1930–2004)** was an Algerian-born French philosopher, who was noted for his development of deconstruction and poststructuralism. One of Derrida's most quoted (and misquoted) phrases was *"il n'y a pas d'hors-texte"*— in other words, there is nothing outside or beyond the text.

16. **Anthony Easthope (1939–1999)** was a professor in English studies at Manchester Metropolitan University, known for his iconoclastic reviews of established critics, as well as his openness to continental philosophy and intellectual innovation.

17. **G. R. Elton (1921–1994)** was a German-born British historian who specialized in the Tudor period, believing that the 1530s saw the development of centralized administration and a "revolution in government." He was fiercely critical of Marxist historians and departures from political or national history.

18. **Niall Ferguson (b. 1964)** is a British historian, particularly known for his

works on financial, international, and imperial history. He is also known for his own media career and role as an advisor to the British government over history teaching in schools.

19. **Fritz Fischer (1908–1999)** was an influential German historian who is most famous for his groundbreaking work on World War I.

20. **Michel Foucault (1926–1984)** was a French philosopher who wrote seminal work on epistemology, discourse, sexuality, and the discipline exercised by social institutions. Foucault is undoubtedly one of the most important thinkers since World War II—and his omission from Richard J. Evans's discussion is striking.

21. **Thomas L. Haskell (b. 1939)** is an American historian who has a particular interest in American history. He is Samuel G. McCann Professor Emeritus of History at Rice University, Houston.

22. **Christopher Hill (1912–2003)** was a British Marxist historian who focused mainly on seventeenth-century Britain and studied the radical groups of democrats and dissenters who flourished during the English Civil War.

23. **Gertrude Himmelfarb (b. 1922)** is an American historian who has written on the intellectual culture of Victorian Britain and calls for a return to traditional and conservative approaches to history.

24. **Lynn Hunt (b. 1945)** is an American historian, known for her works on the French Revolution and the theory of history. She was one of the most prominent champions of the cultural turn in the early 1990s.

25. **David Irving (b. 1938)** is a British author who has gained notoriety for his works on World War II and Nazi Germany. One of the leaders of Holocaust "revisionism," Irving was arrested and imprisoned in 2006 in Austria, where Holocaust denial is illegal.

26. **Keith Jenkins (b. 1943)** is a British postmodern historian and philosopher of history. Jenkins responds to Richard J. Evans in *Why History? Ethics and Postmodernity*.

27. **Ludmilla Jordanova (b. 1949)** is a British historian who is currently a professor at the University of Durham. She has produced works on gender and

medicine in history, as well as a work on the nature of historical practice and the uses of visual culture.

28. **Deborah Lipstadt (b. 1947)** is an American historian noted for her works on the Holocaust. She is the Dorot Professor of Modern Jewish and Holocaust Studies at Emory University, Atlanta.

29. **Peter Mandler (b. 1958)** is professor of history at Cambridge and an expert on British nineteenth-and twentieth-century cultural history. He has written extensively on the development of heritage in modern Britain, as well as the relationship between history and the social sciences.

30. **Doug Munro** is an adjunct professor at the University of Queensland in New Zealand who works on historical biography and the twentieth-century Pacific.

31. **Alun Munslow (b. 1947)** is professor of history at Staffordshire University, known as a champion of postmodern and deconstructionist approaches.

32. **Peter Novick (1934–2012)** is an American historian who is particularly known for his works on the theory of history.

33. **Diane Purkiss (b. 1961)** is an Australian historian who has written about gender and literature, witchcraft, and the English Civil War.

34. **Leopold von Ranke (1795–1886)** was a German historian at the University of Berlin who laid the foundations of source-based criticism and is hence regarded as the father of the discipline. He worked extensively on the history of religion and diplomacy in early modern Europe.

35. **Joan Wallach Scott (b. 1941)** is an American historian based at Princeton. She has published widely on French social and cultural history, and is one of the most important thinkers on gender and feminist history.

36. **Joseph Stalin (1878–1953)** was the head of the Soviet Union, ruling as General Secretary of the Communist Party from 1928 through to his death in 1953.

37. **Lawrence Stone (1919–1999)** was a British historian of the early modern period who taught at Oxford and Princeton. Richard J. Evans cites his notorious

clash with Hugh Trevor-Roper over an article in which Stone had claimed that there was a decline in the economic power of the aristocracy on the eve of the English Civil War—an argument that Trevor-Roper demolished by exposing Stone's misuse and misreading of the sources.

38. **Keith Thomas (b. 1933)** is a British historian who was professor of modern history at Oxford from 1986 to 2000. A pioneer in borrowing methods from anthropology, Thomas has written on magic, superstition, religion, and ideas about nature in early modern Britain.

39. **Thucydides (460–395 B.C.E.)** was one of the greatest Greek historians, author of a devastating history of the Peloponnesian War between Athens and Sparta.

40. **John Tosh** is a British historian who is currently professor of history at Roehampton University. He has gained note for his works on masculinity in history and the nature of history.

41. **G. M. Trevelyan (1876–1962)** was a British historian noted for his works on seventeenth-to nineteenth-century British politics and his espousal of Whig/Liberal ideas. He was also a pioneer in the field of social history, even if Richard J. Evans was dismissive of his literary and patrician approach to the subject.

42. **Hugh Trevor-Roper (1914–2003)** was Regius Professor of Modern History at Oxford. A specialist in early modern Britain and Europe, he was also an early writer on the Third Reich, but his reputation became tarnished through his decision to authenticate bogus Hitler diaries in the 1980s.

43. **Hayden V. White (b. 1928)** is an American historian who has provided many works of historical theory linked to literary criticism. He argues for all historical writing involving a form of narrative "emplotment."

44. **Natalie Zemon-Davis (b. 1928)** is a Canadian-born historian of early modern Europe, famed for her groundbreaking work on women's history, the boundaries between history and anthropology, and the place of fiction and story-telling in the archives.

WORKS CITED

1. Anderson, R. D. "Reviews: In Defence of History." *Scottish Historical Review* 79 (2000): 105–6.

2. Ankersmit, F. R. *Historical Representation*. Stanford, CA: Stanford University Press, 2002.

3. ____. *Narrative Logic: A Semantic Analysis of the Historian's Language*. The Hague: Martinus Nijhoff, 1983.

4. ____. *Sublime Historical Experience*. Stanford, CA: Stanford University Press, 2005.

5. Appleby, Joyce Oldham. "Does It Really Need Defending?" *The Times Literary Supplement*, October 25, 1997.

6. Appleby, Joyce Oldham, Margaret C. Jacob, and Lynn Hunt. *Telling the Truth about History*. New York and London: Norton, 1994.

7. Armitage, David, and Jo Guldi. *The History Manifesto*. Cambridge: Cambridge University Press, 2014. Available online: http://historymanifesto.cambridge.org/.

8. Barthes, Roland. *Image, Music, Text*. Translated by Stephen Heath. London: Flamingo, 1984.

9. Belsey, Catherine. "In Defence of History," *European Journal of English Studies* 3, no. 1 (1999): 106–13.

10. Bentley, Michael. *Modernizing England's Pasts: English Historiography in the Age of Modernism 1870–1970*. Cambridge: Cambridge University Press, 2006.

11. Burrow, John. *A History of Histories: Epics, Chronicles, Romances and Inquiries from Herodotus to the Twentieth Century*. London: Penguin, 2009.

12. Cannadine, David. *G. M. Trevelyan: A Life in History*. London: Fontana, 1993.

13. ____. *What Is History Now?* Basingstoke: Palgrave Macmillan, 2002.

14. Caplan, Jane. *Government without Administration: State and Civil Service in Weimar and Nazi Germany*. Oxford: Clarendon Press, 1989.

15. ____. "Postmodernism, Poststructuralism, and Deconstruction: Notes for

Historians." *Central European History* 22, nos 3–4 (1989): 260–78.

16. Carr, E. H. *What Is History?* Introduced by Richard J. Evans. Fortieth anniversary ed. Basingstoke: Palgrave, 2001.

17. Carr, E. H., and R. W. Davies. *A History of Soviet Russia*. London: Macmillan, 1978.

18. Chakrabarty, Dipesh. *Provincializing Europe: Postcolonial Thought and Historical Difference*. Princeton, N.J.: Princeton University Press, 2000.

19. Collini, Stefan. "The Truth Vandals," *Guardian*, December 18, 1997.

20. Derrida, Jacques. *Of Grammatology*. Translated by Gayatri Chakravorty Spivak. Baltimore and London: Johns Hopkins University Press, 1997.

21. ____. *Writing and Difference*. Translated by Alan Bass. London: Routledge, 2001.

22. Dintenfass, Michael. "Truth's Other: Ethics, the History of the Holocaust, and Historiographical Theory after the Linguistic Turn." *History and Theory* 39, no. 1 (2000): 1–20.

23. Easthope, Anthony. *Textual Practice 12, no. 3* (1998): 563–6.

24. Elton, G. R. *The Practice of History*. Sydney: Methuen, 1967.

25. Evans, Richard J. *The Coming of the Third Reich*. London: Allen Lane, 2003.

26. ____. *Cosmopolitan Islanders: British Historians and the European Continent*. Cambridge: Cambridge University Press, 2009.

27. ____. *Death in Hamburg: Society and Politics in the Cholera Years, 1830–1910*. Oxford: Clarendon Press, 1987.

28. ____. *In Defence of History*. 2nd ed. London: Granta, 2001.

29. ____. *The Feminist Movement in Germany 1894–1933*. London: Sage Publications, 1976.

30. ____. *In Hitler's Shadow: West German Historians and the Attempt to Escape from the Nazi Past*. New York: Pantheon Books, 1989.

31. ____. "The New Nationalism and the Old History: Perspectives on the West German *Historikerstreit*." *Journal of Modern History* 59, no. 4 (1987): 761–97.

32. ____. "Review: *The Annales School: An Intellectual History* by André Burguière." *London Review of Books* 31, no. 23 (December 3, 2009): 12–14.

33. ____. *Rituals of Retribution: Capital Punishment in Germany 1600–1987.* Oxford: Oxford University Press, 1996.

34. ____. *Society and Politics in Wilhelmine Germany.* London: Croom Helm, 1978.

35. ____. *Tales from the German Underworld: Crime and Punishment in the Nineteenth Century.* New Haven, CT, and London: Yale University Press, 1998.

36. ____. *Telling Lies about Hitler: The Holocaust, History and the David Irving Trial.* London: Verso, 2002.

37. ____. *The Third Reich in Power, 1933–1939.* London: Allen Lane, 2005.

38. ____. *The Third Reich at War, 1939–1945.* London: Allen Lane, 2008.

39. Ferguson, Niall. "History Is Dead, Long Live History!" *Sunday Times*, September 21, 1997.

40. ____. *The War of the World: History's Age of Hatred.* London: Allen Lane, 2006.

41. Fischer, Fritz. *War of Illusions: German Policies from 1911 to 1914.* Translated by Marian Jackson. London: Chatto & Windus, 1975.

42. Foucault, Michel. *The Archaeology of Knowledge.* Translated by Alan Sheridan. London: Tavistock Publications, 1972.

43. ____. *The History of Sexuality.* Translated by Robert Hurley. London: Allen Lane, 1979.

44. ____. *The Order of Things: An Archaeology of the Human Sciences.* London: Routledge, 2001.

45. Hamerow, Theodor S. "Guilt, Redemption and Writing German History." *American Historical Review* 88, February (1983): 53–72.

46. Haskell, Thomas L. *Objectivity Is Not Neutrality: Explanatory Schemes in History.* Baltimore and London: Johns Hopkins University Press, 1998.

47. Hill, Christopher. *The Century of Revolution, 1603–1714.* London: Routledge, 2002.

48. ____. *Puritanism and Revolution: Studies in Interpretation of the English Revolution of the Seventeenth Century*. Harmondsworth: Penguin, 1986.

49. Hunt, Lynn. "Does History Need Defending?" *History Workshop Journal* 46, December (1998): 241–9.

50. Hunt, Lynn, Bonnell, Victoria, and Biernacki, Richard, eds. *Beyond the Cultural Turn: New Directions in the Study of Society and Culture*. Berkeley: University of California Press, 1999.

51. Jenkins, Keith. *Re-Thinking History*. With a New Preface and Conversation with the Author by Alun Munslow. London: Routledge, 2003.

52. ____. *On "What Is History?" From Carr and Elton to Rorty and White*. London: Routledge, 1995.

53. ____. *Why History? Ethics and Postmodernity*. London: Routledge, 1999.

54. Jenkins, Keith, and Alun Munslow. *The Nature of History Reader*. London: Routledge, 2004.

55. Jordanova, Ludmilla. *History in Practice*. 2nd ed. London: Hodder Arnold, 2006.

56. Joyce, Patrick. *The Social in Question: New Bearings in History and the Social Sciences*. London: Routledge, 2002.

57. Kenyon, J. P. *The History Men: The Historical Profession in England since the Renaissance*. 2nd ed. London: Weidenfeld & Nicolson, 1993.

58. Lindeman, Mary. "The Discreet Charm of the Diplomatic Archive." *German History: The Journal of the German History Society* 29, no. 2 (1984): 283–304.

59. Lipstadt, Deborah E. *Denying the Holocaust: The Growing Assault on Truth and Memory*. London: Penguin, 1994.

60. ____. *History on Trial: My Day in Court with David Irving*. New York: Harper Perennial, 2006.

61. Macfie, Alexander Lyon. "On the Defence of (My) History." *Rethinking History: The Journal of Theory and Practice* 14, no. 2 (2010): 209–27.

62. Mandler, Peter. *History and National Life*. London: Profile Books, 2002.

63. ____. "The Problem with Cultural History, or is Playtime Over?" *Cultural and Social History* 1, no. 1 (2004): 94–117.

64. Mandler, Peter, and Deborah Cohen. "The History Manifesto: A Critique." *American Historical Review* 120, no. 2 (2015): 530–42.

65. Marx, Karl, and Friedrich Engels. *The Communist Manifesto*. Edited and introduced by Jeffrey C. Isaac. New Haven, CT: Yale University Press, 2012.

66. Marx, Karl, and Hugo Gellert. *Karl Marx' 'Capital'*. Baarle-Nassau: SoMa, 1981.

67. Miller, Daniel, ed. *Materiality*. Durham, NC: Duke University Press, 2005.

68. Munro, Doug. "*In Defence of History* (Review)." *Journal of Social History* 36, no. 1 (2002): 242–4.

69. Munslow, Alun. *Deconstructing History*. 2nd ed. London: Routledge, 2006.

70. ____. *Narrative and History*. Basingstoke: Palgrave Macmillan, 2007.

71. Novick, Peter. *The Holocaust and Collective Memory: The American Experience*. London: Bloomsbury, 2000.

72. ____. *That Noble Dream: The "Objectivity Question" and the American Historical Profession*. Cambridge: Cambridge University Press, 1988.

73. Parkin, Frank. *Marxism and Class Theory: A Bourgeois Critique*. London: Tavistock Publications, 1981, c. 1979.

74. Purdue, A. W. "Book of the Week: Cosmopolitan Islanders." *Times Higher Education*, July 9, 2009. Accessed October 24, 2013. http://www.timeshighereducation.co.uk/407279.article.

75. Purkiss, Diane. "A Response to Richard J. Evans." *History in Focus*. Accessed October 24, 2013. http://www.history.ac.uk/ihr/Focus/Whatishistory/purkiss1.html.

76. ____. *The Witch in History: Early Modern and Twentieth-Century Representations*. London: Routledge, 1996.

77. Ranke, Leopold von. *History of the Latin and Teutonic Nations, 1494 to 1514*. Translated by G.R. Dennis. Introduction by E. Armstrong. London: Bell, 1915.

78. "Richard J. Evans—In Defence of History." *Kirkus Reviews*, November 1, 1998.

79. Samuel, Raphael. *History Workshop: A Collectanea 1967–1991*. London: History Workshop, 1991.

80. ____. *Theatres of Memory: Past and Present in Contemporary Culture*, vol. 1. London: Verso, 1996.

81. Samuel, Raphael, Jennie Kitteringham, and David M. Morgan. *Village Life and Labour*. Edited by Raphael Samuel. London: Routledge & Kegan Paul, 1975.

82. Snowman, Daniel. "Daniel Snowman Meets the Historian of Germany, Defender of History and Expert Witness in the Irving Trial." *History Today* 54 (January 2004): 45–7.

83. Thomas, Keith. *Religion and the Decline of Magic: Studies in Popular Beliefs in Sixteenth-and Seventeenth-Century England*. Harmondsworth: Penguin, 1978.

84. Tosh, John. "Shorter Note: In Defence of History." *The English Historical Review* 114 (1999): 805–6.

85. ____. *Why History Matters*. Basingstoke: Palgrave Macmillan, 2008.

86. Tosh, John, and Sean Lang. *The Pursuit of History: Aims, Methods and New Directions in the Study of Modern History*. 4th ed. Harlow: Longman, 2006.

87. Trevelyan, G. M. *British History in the Nineteenth Century (1782–1939)*. [S.l.]: [s.n.], 1947.

88. ____. *The English Revolution, 1688–1689*. [S.l.]: [s.n.], 1956.

89. Trevor-Roper, H. R. *The Last Days of Hitler*. 7th ed. London: Papermac, 1995.

90. White, Hayden. *The Content of Form: Narrative Discourse and Historical Representation*. Baltimore and London: Johns Hopkins University Press, 1987.

91. ____. *Metahistory: The Historical Imagination in Nineteenth-Century Europe*. Baltimore and London: Johns Hopkins University Press, 1975.

92. ____. *Tropics of Discourse: Essays in Cultural Criticism*. Baltimore and London: Johns Hopkins University Press, 1978.

93. Young, Robert, *White Mythologies: Writing, History and the West*. London: Routledge, 1990.

原书作者简介

理查德·J. 艾文斯爵士是英国最有名望的历史学家之一，1947年出生于伦敦，在牛津大学学习历史，师从当时最著名的思想家，后开创了辉煌的学术生涯。他专攻德国历史，目前是剑桥大学近代史钦定讲座教授。他因撰写有关19世纪德国女权主义、犯罪和疾病的历史学著作而闻名，后创作了著名的第三帝国三部曲。他指出并分析了对历史和历史观念的误用（尤其是对纳粹大屠杀的否定），这使他声名鹊起。他的著作《捍卫历史》也成为历史专业本科生的必读书。

本书作者简介

尼古拉斯·皮尔西博士拥有伦敦大学学院的文化研究博士学位，目前是伦敦大学学院欧洲语言、文化和社会学院荷兰语系的荣誉研究员。

托马斯·斯坦默斯博士是达勒姆大学的近代欧洲史讲师，专门研究法国大革命时期的文化史，研究方向涵盖与18世纪和19世纪欧洲有关的历史编纂学和理论方面的学术争议，著有《收集、回忆和革命：19世纪巴黎旧事拾遗》。

世界名著中的批判性思维

《世界思想宝库钥匙丛书》致力于深入浅出地阐释全世界著名思想家的观点，不论是谁、在何处都能了解到，从而推进批判性思维发展。

《世界思想宝库钥匙丛书》与世界顶尖大学的一流学者合作，为一系列学科中最有影响的著作推出新的分析文本，介绍其观点和影响。在这一不断扩展的系列中，每种选入的著作都代表了历经时间考验的思想典范。通过为这些著作提供必要背景、揭示原作者的学术渊源以及说明这些著作所产生的影响，本系列图书希望让读者以新视角看待这些划时代的经典之作。读者应学会思考、运用并挑战这些著作中的观点，而不是简单接受它们。

ABOUT THE AUTHOR OF THE ORIGINAL WORK

Sir Richard J. Evans is one of Britain's most respected scholars of German history. Born in London in 1947, Evans studied history at Oxford with some of the most respected thinkers of his time, and went on to have a distinguished academic career, eventually becoming Regius Professor of Modern History at Cambridge. He made his name with publications on the history of feminism, crime, and disease in nineteenth-century Germany, before turning to write an influential trilogy on the Third Reich. Evans has also crafted himself a reputation for identifying and analyzing the misuse of history and historical ideas, specifically when it comes to Holocaust denial, and his *In Defence of History* has established itself as one of the texts most widely read by modern undergraduate historians.

ABOUT THE AUTHORS OF THE ANALYSIS

Dr Nicholas Piercey holds a PhD in cultural studies from University College, London. He is currently an Honorary Research Associate in UCL's Department of Dutch in the UCL School of European Languages, Culture & Society.

Dr Thomas Stammers is lecturer in Modern European history at Durham University, where he specialises in the cultural history of France in the age of revolution. He is the author of *Collection, Recollection, Revolution: Scavenging the Past in Nineteenth-Century Paris*. Dr Stammers's research interests include a wide range of historiographical and theoretical controversies related to eighteenth and nineteenth-century Europe.

ABOUT MACAT
GREAT WORKS FOR CRITICAL THINKING

Macat is focused on making the ideas of the world's great thinkers accessible and comprehensible to everybody, everywhere, in ways that promote the development of enhanced critical thinking skills.

It works with leading academics from the world's top universities to produce new analyses that focus on the ideas and the impact of the most influential works ever written across a wide variety of academic disciplines. Each of the works that sit at the heart of its growing library is an enduring example of great thinking. But by setting them in context — and looking at the influences that shaped their authors, as well as the responses they provoked — Macat encourages readers to look at these classics and game-changers with fresh eyes. Readers learn to think, engage and challenge their ideas, rather than simply accepting them.

批判性思维与《捍卫历史》

首要批判性思维技巧：评估

次要批判性思维技巧：理性化思维

理查德·J. 艾文斯创作《捍卫历史》，是因为20世纪80年代到90年代历史学受到该领域"文化转向"的巨大冲击，历史学家被迫直面后现代主义思想。后现代主义观点认为，所有文本都是作者在信息不充分的条件下，发挥自身倾向、偏见的产物，因此谁都没有盖棺论定的特权。根据这一观点，不可能存在客观的历史，只有文本研究而已。

《捍卫历史》探讨了历史学研究方法的各个方面，不过这一著作的重点在于对后现代主义思想进行全面评估。对于后现代主义者提出的思考方式，艾文斯斟酌了其合理性，并发现其存在重大缺陷。他强烈质疑后现代主义观点的适用性和有效性，并试图表明，后现代主义最终将陷入逻辑不能自洽的境地。既然所有的文本都同等有效（或者无效），那么后现代主义者怎么能够宣称他们的主张比其他学派更加"接近真相"呢？艾文斯进一步指出，可以根据后现代主义的这一观点，认为否认纳粹大屠杀的著作与揭露大屠杀史实的著作是同等有效的。他问道，为什么没有后现代主义者敢于这么说呢？不讲情面的评估在学术辩论中多么有用，这就是最好的例子。

CRITICAL THINKING AND *IN DEFENCE OF HISTORY*

- Primary critical thinking skill: EVALUATION
- Secondary critical thinking skill: REASONING

Richard Evans wrote *In Defence of History* at a time when the historian's profession was coming under heavy attack as a result of the "cultural turn" taken by the discipline during the late 1980s and the 1990s. Historians were being forced to face up to postmodern thinking, which argued that, because all texts were the product of biased writers who had incomplete information, none could be privileged above others. In this reading, there could be no objective history, merely the study of the texts themselves.

While *In Defence of History* addresses all aspects of historical method, its key focus is on an extensive evaluation of this postmodern thinking. Evans judges the acceptability of the reasoning advanced by the postmodernists — and finds it badly wanting. He is strongly critical both of the relevance and of the adequacy of their arguments, seeking to show that, ultimately, they are guilty of failing to accept the logic of their own position. All texts are equally valid, or invalid, they suggest — while insisting that the products of their own school are in fact more "true" than those of their opponents. Evans concludes by pointing out that this same argument could be advanced to suggest that the works of Holocaust deniers are just as valid as are those of historians who accept that the Nazis set out to commit genocide. So why, he demands, is no postmodernist willing to say as much? A devastating example of the usefulness of relentless evaluation.

《世界思想宝库钥匙丛书》简介

《世界思想宝库钥匙丛书》致力于为一系列在各领域产生重大影响的人文社科类经典著作提供独特的学术探讨。每一本读物都不仅仅是原经典著作的内容摘要,而是介绍并深入研究原经典著作的学术渊源、主要观点和历史影响。这一丛书的目的是提供一套学习资料,以促进读者掌握批判性思维,从而更全面、深刻地去理解重要思想。

每一本读物分为3个部分:学术渊源、学术思想和学术影响,每个部分下有4个小节。这些章节旨在从各个方面研究原经典著作及其反响。

由于独特的体例,每一本读物不但易于阅读,而且另有一项优点:所有读物的编排体例相同,读者在进行某个知识层面的调查或研究时可交叉参阅多本该丛书中的相关读物,从而开启跨领域研究的路径。

为了方便阅读,每本读物最后还列出了术语表和人名表(在书中则以星号*标记),此外还有参考文献。

《世界思想宝库钥匙丛书》与剑桥大学合作,理清了批判性思维的要点,即如何通过6种技能来进行有效思考。其中3种技能让我们能够理解问题,另3种技能让我们有能力解决问题。这6种技能合称为"批判性思维PACIER模式",它们是:

分析:了解如何建立一个观点;
评估:研究一个观点的优点和缺点;
阐释:对意义所产生的问题加以理解;
创造性思维:提出新的见解,发现新的联系;
解决问题:提出切实有效的解决办法;
理性化思维:创建有说服力的观点。

THE MACAT LIBRARY

The Macat Library is a series of unique academic explorations of seminal works in the humanities and social sciences — books and papers that have had a significant and widely recognised impact on their disciplines. It has been created to serve as much more than just a summary of what lies between the covers of a great book. It illuminates and explores the influences on, ideas of, and impact of that book. Our goal is to offer a learning resource that encourages critical thinking and fosters a better, deeper understanding of important ideas.

Each publication is divided into three Sections: Influences, Ideas, and Impact. Each Section has four Modules. These explore every important facet of the work, and the responses to it.

This Section-Module structure makes a Macat Library book easy to use, but it has another important feature. Because each Macat book is written to the same format, it is possible (and encouraged!) to cross-reference multiple Macat books along the same lines of inquiry or research. This allows the reader to open up interesting interdisciplinary pathways.

To further aid your reading, lists of glossary terms and people mentioned are included at the end of this book (these are indicated by an asterisk [*] throughout) — as well as a list of works cited.

Macat has worked with the University of Cambridge to identify the elements of critical thinking and understand the ways in which six different skills combine to enable effective thinking.

Three allow us to fully understand a problem; three more give us the tools to solve it. Together, these six skills make up the PACIER model of critical thinking. They are:

ANALYSIS — understanding how an argument is built
EVALUATION — exploring the strengths and weaknesses of an argument
INTERPRETATION — understanding issues of meaning
CREATIVE THINKING — coming up with new ideas and fresh connections
PROBLEM-SOLVING — producing strong solutions
REASONING — creating strong arguments

"《世界思想宝库钥匙丛书》提供了独一无二的跨学科学习和研究工具。它介绍那些革新了各自学科研究的经典著作，还邀请全世界一流专家和教育机构进行严谨的分析，为每位读者打开世界顶级教育的大门。"

——安德烈亚斯·施莱歇尔，
经济合作与发展组织教育与技能司司长

"《世界思想宝库钥匙丛书》直面大学教育的巨大挑战……他们组建了一支精干而活跃的学者队伍，来推出在研究广度上颇具新意的教学材料。"

——布罗尔斯教授、勋爵，剑桥大学前校长

"《世界思想宝库钥匙丛书》的愿景令人赞叹。它通过分析和阐释那些曾深刻影响人类思想以及社会、经济发展的经典文本，提供了新的学习方法。它推动批判性思维，这对于任何社会和经济体来说都是至关重要的。这就是未来的学习方法。"

——查尔斯·克拉克阁下，英国前教育大臣

"对于那些影响了各自领域的著作，《世界思想宝库钥匙丛书》能让人们立即了解到围绕那些著作展开的评论性言论，这让该系列图书成为在这些领域从事研究的师生们不可或缺的资源。"

——威廉·特朗佐教授，加利福尼亚大学圣地亚哥分校

"Macat offers an amazing first-of-its-kind tool for interdisciplinary learning and research. Its focus on works that transformed their disciplines and its rigorous approach, drawing on the world's leading experts and educational institutions, opens up a world-class education to anyone."

—— Andreas Schleicher, Director for Education and Skills, Organisation for Economic Co-operation and Development

"Macat is taking on some of the major challenges in university education... They have drawn together a strong team of active academics who are producing teaching materials that are novel in the breadth of their approach."

—— Prof Lord Broers, former Vice-Chancellor of the University of Cambridge

"The Macat vision is exceptionally exciting. It focuses upon new modes of learning which analyse and explain seminal texts which have profoundly influenced world thinking and so social and economic development. It promotes the kind of critical thinking which is essential for any society and economy. This is the learning of the future."

—— Rt Hon Charles Clarke, former UK Secretary of State for Education

"The Macat analyses provide immediate access to the critical conversation surrounding the books that have shaped their respective discipline, which will make them an invaluable resource to all of those, students and teachers, working in the field."

—— Prof William Tronzo, University of California at San Diego

The Macat Library
世界思想宝库钥匙丛书

TITLE	中文书名	类别
An Analysis of Arjun Appadurai's *Modernity at Large: Cultural Dimensions of Globalization*	解析阿尔君·阿帕杜莱《消失的现代性：全球化的文化维度》	人类学
An Analysis of Claude Lévi-Strauss's *Structural Anthropology*	解析克劳德·列维-斯特劳斯《结构人类学》	人类学
An Analysis of Marcel Mauss's *The Gift*	解析马塞尔·莫斯《礼物》	人类学
An Analysis of Jared M. Diamond's *Guns, Germs, and Steel: The Fate of Human Societies*	解析贾雷德·M.戴蒙德《枪炮、病菌与钢铁：人类社会的命运》	人类学
An Analysis of Clifford Geertz's *The Interpretation of Cultures*	解析克利福德·格尔茨《文化的解释》	人类学
An Analysis of Philippe Ariès's *Centuries of Childhood: A Social History of Family Life*	解析菲利浦·阿利埃斯《儿童的世纪：旧制度下的儿童和家庭生活》	人类学
An Analysis of W. Chan Kim & Renée Mauborgne's *Blue Ocean Strategy*	解析金伟灿/勒妮·莫博涅《蓝海战略》	商业
An Analysis of John P. Kotter's *Leading Change*	解析约翰·P.科特《领导变革》	商业
An Analysis of Michael E. Porter's *Competitive Strategy: Techniques for Analyzing Industries and Competitors*	解析迈克尔·E.波特《竞争战略：分析产业和竞争对手的技术》	商业
An Analysis of Jean Lave & Etienne Wenger's *Situated Learning: Legitimate Peripheral Participation*	解析琼·莱夫/艾蒂纳·温格《情境学习：合法的边缘性参与》	商业
An Analysis of Douglas McGregor's *The Human Side of Enterprise*	解析道格拉斯·麦格雷戈《企业的人性面》	商业
An Analysis of Milton Friedman's *Capitalism and Freedom*	解析米尔顿·弗里德曼《资本主义与自由》	商业
An Analysis of Ludwig von Mises's *The Theory of Money and Credit*	解析路德维希·冯·米塞斯《货币和信用理论》	经济学
An Analysis of Adam Smith's *The Wealth of Nations*	解析亚当·斯密《国富论》	经济学
An Analysis of Thomas Piketty's *Capital in the Twenty-First Century*	解析托马斯·皮凯蒂《21世纪资本论》	经济学
An Analysis of Nassim Nicholas Taleb's *The Black Swan: The Impact of the Highly Improbable*	解析纳西姆·尼古拉斯·塔勒布《黑天鹅：如何应对不可预知的未来》	经济学
An Analysis of Ha-Joon Chang's *Kicking Away the Ladder*	解析张夏准《富国陷阱：发达国家为何踢开梯子》	经济学
An Analysis of Thomas Robert Malthus's *An Essay on the Principle of Population*	解析托马斯·罗伯特·马尔萨斯《人口论》	经济学

An Analysis of John Maynard Keynes's *The General Theory of Employment, Interest and Money*	解析约翰·梅纳德·凯恩斯《就业、利息和货币通论》	经济学
An Analysis of Milton Friedman's *The Role of Monetary Policy*	解析米尔顿·弗里德曼《货币政策的作用》	经济学
An Analysis of Burton G. Malkiel's *A Random Walk Down Wall Street*	解析伯顿·G. 马尔基尔《漫步华尔街》	经济学
An Analysis of Friedrich A. Hayek's *The Road to Serfdom*	解析弗里德里希·A. 哈耶克《通往奴役之路》	经济学
An Analysis of Charles P. Kindleberger's *Manias, Panics, and Crashes: A History of Financial Crises*	解析查尔斯·P. 金德尔伯格《疯狂、惊恐和崩溃：金融危机史》	经济学
An Analysis of Amartya Sen's *Development as Freedom*	解析阿马蒂亚·森《以自由看待发展》	经济学
An Analysis of Rachel Carson's *Silent Spring*	解析蕾切尔·卡森《寂静的春天》	地理学
An Analysis of Charles Darwin's *On the Origin of Species: by Means of Natural Selection, or The Preservation of Favoured Races in the Struggle for Life*	解析查尔斯·达尔文《物种起源》	地理学
An Analysis of World Commission on Environment and Development's *The Brundtland Report: Our Common Future*	解析世界环境与发展委员会《布伦特兰报告：我们共同的未来》	地理学
An Analysis of James E. Lovelock's *Gaia: A New Look at Life on Earth*	解析詹姆斯·E. 拉伍洛克《盖娅：地球生命的新视野》	地理学
An Analysis of Paul Kennedy's *The Rise and Fall of the Great Powers: Economic Change and Military Conflict from 1500–2000*	解析保罗·肯尼迪《大国的兴衰：1500—2000年的经济变革与军事冲突》	历史
An Analysis of Janet L. Abu-Lughod's *Before European Hegemony: The World System A. D. 1250–1350*	解析珍妮特·L. 阿布-卢格霍德《欧洲霸权之前：1250—1350年的世界体系》	历史
An Analysis of Alfred W. Crosby's *The Columbian Exchange: Biological and Cultural Consequences of 1492*	解析艾尔弗雷德·W. 克罗斯比《哥伦布大交换：1492年以后的生物影响和文化冲击》	历史
An Analysis of Tony Judt's *Postwar: A History of Europe since 1945*	解析托尼·朱特《战后欧洲史》	历史
An Analysis of Richard J. Evans's *In Defence of History*	解析理查德·J. 艾文斯《捍卫历史》	历史
An Analysis of Eric Hobsbawm's *The Age of Revolution: Europe 1789–1848*	解析艾瑞克·霍布斯鲍姆《革命的年代：欧洲 1789—1848年》	历史

An Analysis of Roland Barthes's *Mythologies*	解析罗兰·巴特《神话学》	文学与批判理论
An Analysis of Simone de Beauvoir's *The Second Sex*	解析西蒙娜·德·波伏娃《第二性》	文学与批判理论
An Analysis of Edward W. Said's *Orientalism*	解析爱德华·W.萨义德《东方主义》	文学与批判理论
An Analysis of Virginia Woolf's *A Room of One's Own*	解析弗吉尼亚·伍尔芙《一间自己的房间》	文学与批判理论
An Analysis of Judith Butler's *Gender Trouble*	解析朱迪斯·巴特勒《性别麻烦》	文学与批判理论
An Analysis of Ferdinand de Saussure's *Course in General Linguistics*	解析费尔迪南·德·索绪尔《普通语言学教程》	文学与批判理论
An Analysis of Susan Sontag's *On Photography*	解析苏珊·桑塔格《论摄影》	文学与批判理论
An Analysis of Walter Benjamin's *The Work of Art in the Age of Mechanical Reproduction*	解析瓦尔特·本雅明《机械复制时代的艺术作品》	文学与批判理论
An Analysis of W. E. B. Du Bois's *The Souls of Black Folk*	解析W.E.B.杜波依斯《黑人的灵魂》	文学与批判理论
An Analysis of Plato's *The Republic*	解析柏拉图《理想国》	哲学
An Analysis of Plato's *Symposium*	解析柏拉图《会饮篇》	哲学
An Analysis of Aristotle's *Metaphysics*	解析亚里士多德《形而上学》	哲学
An Analysis of Aristotle's *Nicomachean Ethics*	解析亚里士多德《尼各马可伦理学》	哲学
An Analysis of Immanuel Kant's *Critique of Pure Reason*	解析伊曼努尔·康德《纯粹理性批判》	哲学
An Analysis of Ludwig Wittgenstein's *Philosophical Investigations*	解析路德维希·维特根斯坦《哲学研究》	哲学
An Analysis of G. W. F. Hegel's *Phenomenology of Spirit*	解析G.W.F.黑格尔《精神现象学》	哲学
An Analysis of Baruch Spinoza's *Ethics*	解析巴鲁赫·斯宾诺莎《伦理学》	哲学
An Analysis of Hannah Arendt's *The Human Condition*	解析汉娜·阿伦特《人的境况》	哲学
An Analysis of G. E. M. Anscombe's *Modern Moral Philosophy*	解析G. E. M. 安斯康姆《现代道德哲学》	哲学
An Analysis of David Hume's *An Enquiry Concerning Human Understanding*	解析大卫·休谟《人类理解研究》	哲学

An Analysis of Søren Kierkegaard's *Fear and Trembling*	解析索伦·克尔凯郭尔《恐惧与战栗》	哲学
An Analysis of René Descartes's *Meditations on First Philosophy*	解析勒内·笛卡尔《第一哲学沉思录》	哲学
An Analysis of Friedrich Nietzsche's *On the Genealogy of Morality*	解析弗里德里希·尼采《论道德的谱系》	哲学
An Analysis of Gilbert Ryle's *The Concept of Mind*	解析吉尔伯特·赖尔《心的概念》	哲学
An Analysis of Thomas Kuhn's *The Structure of Scientific Revolutions*	解析托马斯·库恩《科学革命的结构》	哲学
An Analysis of John Stuart Mill's *Utilitarianism*	解析约翰·斯图亚特·穆勒《功利主义》	哲学
An Analysis of Aristotle's *Politics*	解析亚里士多德《政治学》	政治学
An Analysis of Niccolò Machiavelli's *The Prince*	解析尼科洛·马基雅维利《君主论》	政治学
An Analysis of Karl Marx's *Capital*	解析卡尔·马克思《资本论》	政治学
An Analysis of Benedict Anderson's *Imagined Communities*	解析本尼迪克特·安德森《想象的共同体》	政治学
An Analysis of Samuel P. Huntington's *The Clash of Civilizations and the Remaking of World Order*	解析塞缪尔·P.亨廷顿《文明的冲突与世界秩序的重建》	政治学
An Analysis of Alexis de Tocqueville's *Democracy in America*	解析阿列克西·德·托克维尔《论美国的民主》	政治学
An Analysis of John A. Hobson's *Imperialism: A Study*	解析约翰·A.霍布森《帝国主义》	政治学
An Analysis of Thomas Paine's *Common Sense*	解析托马斯·潘恩《常识》	政治学
An Analysis of John Rawls's *A Theory of Justice*	解析约翰·罗尔斯《正义论》	政治学
An Analysis of Francis Fukuyama's *The End of History and the Last Man*	解析弗朗西斯·福山《历史的终结与最后的人》	政治学
An Analysis of John Locke's *Two Treatises of Government*	解析约翰·洛克《政府论》	政治学
An Analysis of Sun Tzu's *The Art of War*	解析孙武《孙子兵法》	政治学
An Analysis of Henry Kissinger's *World Order: Reflections on the Character of Nations and the Course of History*	解析亨利·基辛格《世界秩序》	政治学
An Analysis of Jean-Jacques Rousseau's *The Social Contract*	解析让-雅克·卢梭《社会契约论》	政治学

English Title	中文标题	学科
An Analysis of Odd Arne Westad's *The Global Cold War: Third World Interventions and the Making of Our Times*	解析文安立《全球冷战：美苏对第三世界的干涉与当代世界的形成》	政治学
An Analysis of Sigmund Freud's *The Interpretation of Dreams*	解析西格蒙德·弗洛伊德《梦的解析》	心理学
An Analysis of William James' *The Principles of Psychology*	解析威廉·詹姆斯《心理学原理》	心理学
An Analysis of Philip Zimbardo's *The Lucifer Effect*	解析菲利普·津巴多《路西法效应》	心理学
An Analysis of Leon Festinger's *A Theory of Cognitive Dissonance*	解析利昂·费斯汀格《认知失调论》	心理学
An Analysis of Richard H. Thaler & Cass R. Sunstein's *Nudge: Improving Decisions about Health, Wealth, and Happiness*	解析理查德·H. 泰勒/卡斯·R. 桑斯坦《助推：如何做出有关健康、财富和幸福的更优决策》	心理学
An Analysis of Gordon Allport's *The Nature of Prejudice*	解析高尔登·奥尔波特《偏见的本质》	心理学
An Analysis of Steven Pinker's *The Better Angels of Our Nature: Why Violence Has Declined*	解析斯蒂芬·平克《人性中的善良天使：暴力为什么会减少》	心理学
An Analysis of Stanley Milgram's *Obedience to Authority*	解析斯坦利·米尔格拉姆《对权威的服从》	心理学
An Analysis of Betty Friedan's *The Feminine Mystique*	解析贝蒂·弗里丹《女性的奥秘》	心理学
An Analysis of David Riesman's *The Lonely Crowd: A Study of the Changing American Character*	解析大卫·理斯曼《孤独的人群：美国人社会性格演变之研究》	社会学
An Analysis of Franz Boas's *Race, Language and Culture*	解析弗朗兹·博厄斯《种族、语言与文化》	社会学
An Analysis of Pierre Bourdieu's *Outline of a Theory of Practice*	解析皮埃尔·布尔迪厄《实践理论大纲》	社会学
An Analysis of Max Weber's *The Protestant Ethic and the Spirit of Capitalism*	解析马克斯·韦伯《新教伦理与资本主义精神》	社会学
An Analysis of Jane Jacobs's *The Death and Life of Great American Cities*	解析简·雅各布斯《美国大城市的死与生》	社会学
An Analysis of C. Wright Mills's *The Sociological Imagination*	解析C. 赖特·米尔斯《社会学的想象力》	社会学
An Analysis of Robert E. Lucas Jr.'s *Why Doesn't Capital Flow from Rich to Poor Countries?*	解析小罗伯特·E. 卢卡斯《为何资本不从富国流向穷国？》	社会学

An Analysis of Émile Durkheim's *On Suicide*	解析埃米尔·迪尔凯姆《自杀论》	社会学
An Analysis of Eric Hoffer's *The True Believer: Thoughts on the Nature of Mass Movements*	解析埃里克·霍弗《狂热分子：群众运动圣经》	社会学
An Analysis of Jared M. Diamond's *Collapse: How Societies Choose to Fail or Survive*	解析贾雷德·M.戴蒙德《大崩溃：社会如何选择兴亡》	社会学
An Analysis of Michel Foucault's *The History of Sexuality Vol. 1: The Will to Knowledge*	解析米歇尔·福柯《性史（第一卷）：求知意志》	社会学
An Analysis of Michel Foucault's *Discipline and Punish*	解析米歇尔·福柯《规训与惩罚》	社会学
An Analysis of Richard Dawkins's *The Selfish Gene*	解析理查德·道金斯《自私的基因》	社会学
An Analysis of Antonio Gramsci's *Prison Notebooks*	解析安东尼奥·葛兰西《狱中札记》	社会学
An Analysis of Augustine's *Confessions*	解析奥古斯丁《忏悔录》	神学
An Analysis of C. S. Lewis's *The Abolition of Man*	解析C. S.路易斯《人之废》	神学

图书在版编目（CIP）数据

解析理查德·J.艾文斯《捍卫历史》/尼古拉斯·皮尔西（Nicholas Piercey），托马斯·斯坦默斯（Thomas Stammers）著；李文中译. —上海：上海外语教育出版社，2021
（世界思想宝库钥匙丛书）
ISBN 978-7-5446-6758-6

Ⅰ.①解… Ⅱ.①尼… ②托… ③李… Ⅲ.①史学－研究 Ⅳ.①K0

中国版本图书馆CIP数据核字（2021）第043930号

This Chinese-English bilingual edition of *An Analysis of Richard J. Evans's In Defence of History* is published by arrangement with Macat International Limited.
Licensed for sale throughout the world.

本书汉英双语版由Macat国际有限公司授权上海外语教育出版社有限公司出版。
供在全世界范围内发行、销售。

图字：09－2018－549

出版发行：上海外语教育出版社
　　　　　（上海外国语大学内）　邮编：200083
电　　话：021-65425300（总机）
电子邮箱：bookinfo@sflep.com.cn
网　　址：http://www.sflep.com
责任编辑：梁瀚杰

印　　刷：上海信老印刷厂
开　　本：890×1240　1/32　印张 6.25　字数 129千字
版　　次：2021年7月第1版　2021年7月第1次印刷

书　　号：ISBN 978-7-5446-6758-6
定　　价：30.00 元

本版图书如有印装质量问题，可向本社调换
质量服务热线：4008-213-263　电子邮箱：editorial@sflep.com